# EXPLORING
# THE SOLE

C000178022

*Countryside Books' walking guides cover most areas of
England and Wales and include the following series:*

*County Rambles*
*Walks for Motorists*
*Exploring Long Distance Paths*
*Literary Walks*
*Pub Walks*

*A complete list is available from the publishers.*

# EXPLORING
# THE SOLENT WAY

Anne-Marie Edwards

**COUNTRYSIDE BOOKS**
NEWBURY, BERKSHIRE

First published 1994
© Anne-Marie Edwards 1994

All rights reserved. No reproduction
permitted without the prior permission
of the publishers:

COUNTRYSIDE BOOKS
3 Catherine Road
Newbury, Berkshire

ISBN 1 85306 272 3

Cover photograph of the ferry at Hamble taken by Mike Edwards.
Maps by Bob Carr

Typeset by Textype Typesetters, Cambridge
Produced through MRM Associates Ltd., Reading
Printed in England

# Acknowledgements

It is a pleasure to thank the following people for their help and encouragement:

Mr Colin Piper, Rights of Way Manager, Hampshire County Council

The staff at the Christchurch Information Centre whose enthusiasm was a great encouragement

Mrs M. Stancliffe at Lymington Tourist Centre and Helen Theobald of the Lymington Guided Walks Association

The Westwood Rangers, Hampshire County Council, for information on Westwood Woodland Park and for the map drawn by John Bradman

Roy Underdown, Captain Dickie Snell and Andrew Blyth for information about Hamble and Warsash

Richard Sanders for information about Southsea Castle

The staff of Havant Tourist Information Centre who introduced me to 'twittens'

Peter Holloway and Trish Furse for encouragement and help with the Christchurch walks especially around Steamer Point and Stanpit Marsh

Finally I thank my husband Mike for being my companion on every step of the Way.

# Contents

THE SOLENT WAY

# Introduction

To walk the Solent Way is a unique experience. It is a journey through time. England has always been a maritime nation and the creeks and harbours of Hampshire's coast have witnessed the greatest events in the Country's history. For most of the Way you are rarely out of sight and sound of the sea which for 2,000 years has been a highway for the nation's commerce, a rampart for its defence and a source of livelihood. Increasingly today this fascinating coast is under pressure from industry and the demands of recreation. But the care taken by responsible bodies and organisations of the more vulnerable areas has ensured that this splendid walk is not only interesting, but also for most of the route still beautiful and exceptionally rich in wildlife.

The Solent Way long distance coastal path was established by Hampshire County Council in 1982. Since then the route has been extended and improved and now runs for over 70 miles from near Christchurch (just over the border in Dorset) to Emsworth on the border with Sussex. Further improvements are planned around Pylewell Park (just east of Lymington) and across Beaulieu Heath. I have indicated on the maps, and in the text, the extent of this possible rerouting and the points where new waymarking signs may be expected.

Within the relatively short distance of the Way there is remarkable variety. The bird-haunted marshes of Keyhaven and Pennington, the remote nature reserves around Warsash and Titchfield Haven, and the wide heaths and ancient woodlands of the New Forest form a striking contrast with the historic waterfronts of Southampton and Portsmouth and bustling riverside villages like Hamble, colourful with fishing boats and yachts.

People have visited and settled this attractive coast since earliest times. Flint tools and axes have been found which indicate that man may have been here some 300,000 years ago, before the last Ice Age. As the ice retreated and the climate grew warmer, woodland spread over the area and bands of hunters returned about 12,500 years ago. At that time, southern Britain was linked by dry land to the European continent, a ridge of chalk joined Purbeck with the Isle of Wight and in the place of the Solent a great river ran from west to east. The river deposited gravel terraces both above and below present sea levels where the first permanent settlements were made. Their stone axes are often found. Sea levels continued to rise and about 7,000 years ago the sea breached the chalk ridge, drowned the Solent river and flooded the river valleys, creating the coastline we would recognise today.

Subsequently, waves of invaders have settled these shores, leaving tangible signs of their presence along the Solent Way. The remains of a flourishing port built by Iron Age tribes trading to Ireland, the Mediterranean and the Baltic have been excavated at Hengistbury Head. The Romans were among the first to build sea walls and enclose areas of saltmarsh to make salt pans, initiating an industry which flourished along the Solent shore until the middle of the 19th century, leaving visible traces today. The Saxons have left their work in the street plans of old towns such as Christchurch and ancient churches like St Peter's in Titchfield.

With the coming of the Normans Southampton prospered as a leading commercial port, a position the city still holds. The sheltered waters of the Solent and Spithead made an ideal haven for the fleet and the Tudors began the construction of a great chain of castles and forts, including Hurst and Southsea, built to defend the Solent shore and to ring the main naval base at Portsmouth. Stones to build them were often taken from the churches and abbeys destroyed at the Dissolution whose ruins now grace the Way at Beaulieu, Netley and Titchfield. Villages like Bucklers Hard and Bursledon recall the days when the ships which formed Britain's 'wooden walls' were built on their slipways.

Today, the spread of residential and industrial development has increased man's effect on the coast but surprisingly large areas of Hampshire's natural shoreline have survived. The marshes, heaths and grasslands are specially rich in birdlife and rare plants. As you walk the Solent Way, the sea, framed by the Isle of Wight hills, presents everchanging contrasts of light and shade. There are still remote places where the only sounds you will hear are the murmuring of the waves on the beach or the cries of curlews over the marshes.

This book can be used in two ways. Following the route of the Solent Way, I have devised 14 circular walks which incorporate part of the Way and also explore some of the surrounding countryside. These include rambles around Christchurch's lovely harbour and the still medieval landscape of the New Forest, also walks to some of the delightful villages in the Meon valley and beside the Hamble river. The book can also be used as a guide to the full 70 mile route as there are special notes linking each section.

The rights of way in this book pass through a wide variety of landscapes. I have tried to write a text of simple but careful directions which should be sufficient guides in themselves, but a basic sketch map also accompanies each walk.

The sketch maps are designed as guides to the starting points of the circular walks and they provide an overall view of the routes to be taken. However, the sketch maps are not fully drawn to scale and you are recommended to carry the relevant Ordnance Survey map in the 1:50 000 series with you for more complete and precise mapping detail.

Here is a final note on what to wear and what to take with you. I have found that the great variety of habitats that makes the coast such a splendid place for wildlife – the marshes, shingle banks, reed beds and sea walls – makes strong footwear, even wellingtons, essential. I have recorded cafés, restaurants and pubs along the walks but some of the loveliest places are still remote enough to be without them. Carry snacks with you, especially when walking in the New Forest. The coast is a birdwatcher's paradise, so remember your binoculars.

Anne-Marie Edwards
Ashurst, 1994

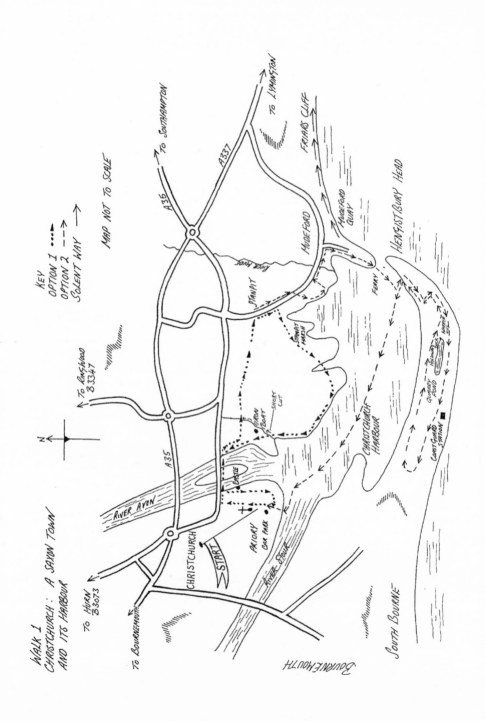

WALK 1
CHRISTCHURCH: A SAXON TOWN
AND ITS HARBOUR

KEY
OPTION 1 ••••►
OPTION 2 ——►
SOLENT WAY ——►

MAP NOT TO SCALE

N

To RINGWOOD
B3347

To BOURNEMOUTH

To HURN
B3073

A35

RIVER AVON

CHRISTCHURCH

PRIORY

CAR PARK

START

RIVER STOUR

BOURNEMOUTH

SOUTH BOURNE

CASTLE

IRON
BOAT

SHORT
CUT

River Avon

STANPIT

A337

A35

To SOUTHAMPTON

To LYMINGTON

FRIARS CLIFF

MUDEFORD

MUDEFORD
QUAY

HENGISTBURY HEAD

STANPIT
MARSH

CHRISTCHURCH HARBOUR

FERRY

QUARRY
POND

COASTGUARD
STATION

# Christchurch: a Saxon town and its harbour – to Stanpit Marsh, Mudeford Quay and Hengistbury Head

**Introduction:** The best place to begin a walk along the Solent shore is Christchurch, a historic town established by Saxon settlers before AD 900. It was an ideal site, at the head of an almost landlocked harbour and protected to the west by the natural rampart of Hengistbury Head.

Today, Christchurch still has the feel of a small Saxon town. Picturesque narrow streets cluster around a ruined castle and tree-shaded walks lead down to the riverside mill built of Saxon stones. Dominating the town and the harbour is Christchurch's splendid Priory Church.

After exploring Christchurch, this walk offers several options depending on the harbour ferry services which only operate in summer. The route around Stanpit Marsh, a nature reserve forming the northern shore of the harbour, can be enjoyed at all times of the year. In summer, you can take the longer walk which continues from the marsh to Mudeford Quay and crosses by ferry to Hengistbury Head, one of the finest viewpoints on the south coast. I suggest a short circular walk on the Head to enjoy its history and wildlife. From the ferry terminal on Hengistbury Head you could return to Mudeford Quay and walk back across the marsh, or take the ferry for an enjoyable harbour trip back to Christchurch Town Quay. All these options are described in the text.

**Distance:** Circular walk (Option 1) Stanpit Marsh 2.5 miles. Circular walk (Option 2) Mudeford Quay and Hengistbury Head, returning to Christchurch by ferry, 4 miles. Optional walk on Hengistbury Head 1.5 miles. OS Landranger series 1:50 000 map 195 Bournemouth, Purbeck and surrounding area or OS Outdoor Leisure series 1:25 000 map 22 New Forest.

**Refreshments:** Christchurch has excellent cafés and restaurants, Mudeford Quay has a café, inn and fish stall, and there are cafés opposite the ferry landing on Hengistbury Head and at Double Dykes.

**How to get there:** The walk starts from Town Quay car park, close to the Priory. From the A35, follow the signs for Christchurch Quay. Turn right in front of the pedestrian precinct in front of the Priory, then after a few yards, turn left to drive into the car park, which is straight ahead.

**The Walk:** From Christchurch Quay car park the walk passes some of the most attractive and historic places in this lovely old town. Beside the car park, dwarfing the narrow streets which link their arms around it, is Christchurch's magnificent Priory Church. The Church dates from 1094 and was part of the monastic buildings completed after 1150 for the Augustinian or Black Canons. At the dissolution of the monasteries in 1539, the Priory was suppressed and most of the buildings destroyed. But the Church survived, claimed by the town as its parish church.

With the Priory on your right, leave the car park by the main gates. The old house at the southern entrance to the Priory was the porter's lodge, one of the few small monastic buildings not destroyed. Ahead, down Quay Street, you will find The Red House, a fascinating museum revealing the whole story of this area from the first settlers on Hengistbury Head 11,000 years ago to the present day. Other galleries are devoted to geology and wildlife.

From just past the car park entrance, turn right to walk diagonally across the churchyard to the iron gates leading to Church Street, a double row of attractive colour-washed Georgian cottages. Walk down Church Street and turn right to continue along Castle Street. At the entrance to the Priory Gardens, you pass a half-timbered, thatched building inscribed 'twelfth century'. Originally this was the Old Court House where the mayor and town dignitaries took their oath of office. Now it houses the New Forest Perfumery. Beside the old house are the stocks and whipping post.

Standing high on an artificial mound beyond the Perfumery are the ruins of the keep of the Norman castle – built to last with walls ten feet thick – and beside the Mill stream there is a rare example of 12th century domestic architecture, the Constable's House, added to the castle for the resident warden. Although the house is now roofless, the walls are almost intact and some of the window openings retain their delicate tracery. An interesting feature is the tall round chimney.

Cross the two bridges where the Avon divides around an island and turn right immediately after the second bridge into Bridge Street car park. Keep straight on leaving the Civic Offices on your left. Now walk diagonally left over the car park behind the offices, following the sign for the leisure centre. Bear left, as the sign directs, along the path past the leisure centre, then keep straight on along the edge of the centre car park towards a blue 'cycling' sign. A good path now leads you beside a stream overhung with willows and in season fringed with irises and kingcups. A golf course is over the rise on your right. The path bears left over the tiny Purewell stream and continues past the recreation ground to the car park adjoining the Stanpit–Mudeford road. The entrance to Stanpit Marsh leads from the car park. Now you have a choice of routes. You could, if you wish, turn right along the road and continue to Mudeford Quay, or you may prefer to visit the marsh first. There is a short return route over the marsh to the Stanpit–Mudeford road, indicated below.

**Option 1 – Stanpit Marsh:** Turn right over the car park, and right again following the footpath to Stanpit Marsh, leaving the scout hut on your right. An inviting path beside a thick hedgerow leads past two wooden gates into the nature reserve.

A wide, very flat expanse of saltmarsh stretches before you, criss-crossed by narrow channels alive with birds. The ground is so flat that you have an uninterrupted view of them all, including herons poised like statues beside the water and golden and grey plovers pecking at the mud with their short beaks. Looking west, the marshes extend so far that it seems you could walk dry-shod to climb the steep slopes of Hengistbury Head outlined against the sky. The harbour contracts to a narrow channel at this point.

Keep straight on past the information caravan to cross one of the slightly higher, sandy areas of the marsh, North Scrubs. This is home to a variety of small animals and familiar garden and woodland birds. In summer small pools attract dragonflies and flowers include mallows, honeysuckle and meadow sweet.

Over a small stream, the ground rises on the left to form Crouch Hill. Excavations here revealed an Early Bronze Age cremation urn and pottery dating from the New Stone Age. A thoughtfully placed seat on the hill provides a wonderful view of the harbour, especially southwards to the narrow entrance between Mudeford Quay – look for a group of black buildings – and the low sandbanks beneath the cliffs of Hengistbury Head.

The path leads across a Bailey bridge over Mother Sillers Channel – named after a notorious 18th century smuggling family who, like many others, made profitable use of these marshes – down to the harbour shore and bears right beside Grimmery Bank. In summer look for damselflies darting across the water of the small pool behind the bank.

The path bears right again beside the estuary of the Purewell stream towards a wreck known as 'the iron boat' presumably cast up here by a storm or very high tide. If the tide is high and the ground very wet return to our earlier path by walking past the boat and beside the Purewell stream. Turn left along your original path and retrace your steps to the main road to cross the Avon bridges and return along Convent Walk as described after the route over Priory Marsh.

To return by a quick route to the Stanpit–Mudeford road, take the path past the iron boat and at the crosstrack turn right to the marsh entrance.

If the ground is dry enough, it is more interesting to return to Christchurch across Priory Marsh. About a hundred yards before you reach the iron boat, turn left and cross the bridge over the Purewell stream. Follow the wooden causeways as they curve right over Priory Marsh, which is entirely freshwater and in season rich in meadow flowers such as water speedwells and flowering rushes.

Leave Priory Marsh and turn left over a stile where you meet a wider footpath and keep straight on to cross the car park behind the

Civic Offices. With the offices on your right, retrace your steps over Bridge Street car park and turn left to cross the Avon bridges. Immediately after the second bridge leave the road and turn left to follow Convent Walk, a lovely path running between the swiftly flowing Avon river and the mill stream curving round the foot of the Priory Gardens, giving views of the Constable's House and the east end of the Priory.

Soon you come to a small medieval bridge on your right and ahead another of Christchurch's historic buildings, Place Mill. The mill was mentioned in the Domesday Book and the large stones at the base of the walls are Saxon. Though part of the monastic buildings, it was too useful to be destroyed and continued to grind corn until 1908. The mill has been purchased by the council and carefully restored. It is open for visitors in the summer.

Turn right over the bridge and take the narrow footpath straight ahead signposted to the Tricycle Museum, leading into Christchurch Quay car park. The Tricycle Museum is on your left.

**Option 2 – Mudeford Quay and Hengistbury Head (Ferries to Hengistbury Head and from the Head to Christchurch Town Quay run in summer only.)** From the car park at the entrance to Stanpit Marsh, continue down the road towards Mudeford. After about 50 yards look across a small green on the right where a plaque marks the site of Tutton's Well, known to the Romans when they landed in AD 43. The water was said to be of 'uncommon purity' so it is possible that it gave its name to the village of Purewell nearby.

Turn right after about ¼ mile following the public footpath sign and bear left along the harbour shore. Now there is a glorious view over the harbour west to Hengistbury Head with the faint outline of the Purbeck Hills beyond. This is a world of small boats, bobbing gently at anchor in the shallow water or pulled up on the shingle beach and piled with lobster pots.

The path leads to a public slipway. Turn left to follow Argyle Road back to the main road and continue towards Mudeford. Cross the little Mude river and, shortly after, you come to a narrow road on the right leading to Mudeford Quay. This was once the centre of Mudeford village and the site of the old ice house – and the correct place to post your letters, proved by a Victorian pillar box with a vertical slit, still standing proudly on the corner.

Turn right down the narrow road to follow the harbour shore to Mudeford Quay, a splendidly natural place noisy with the screeching of gulls and the ceaseless tapping of unfrapped halyards. It still has the aura of an old fishing port with its black and white cottages and old inn where tales are told of smuggling days. Between the quay and the sands of Hengistbury Head is 'the run' where the tide rips in and out of the narrow harbour entrance and rocks the fishing boats lying against the sea wall. The famous Christchurch salmon are netted here in the springtime.

The Solent Way turns left from the quay and follows the coast to Barton on Sea. The walk continues by ferry to Hengistbury Head.

From the ferry landing the sandy spit lined with beach huts runs to the foot of the headland. Follow the harbour shore, or walk between the huts to the beach, past Holloway's Dock. Ironstone boulders (known as 'doggers') are abundant on Hengistbury Head and the dock was made by Mr Holloway's mining company, formed in 1848 and active for about 25 years.

Climb the steps to the top of the headland for a splendid view, west to the chalk cliffs of Ballard Down and Old Harry rocks, south to the West Wight downs and the Needles, and east over Christchurch Harbour laid like a map at your feet. For more views of Poole Harbour entrance and the Purbeck Hills turn left and take the path round the western edge of the headland towards the coastguard's station. Here flint tools left by a party of reindeer hunters some 12,500 years ago have been found. At that time, Britain was still joined to the European continent and from the treeless, tundra-covered slopes of the headland, the hunters looked south over a great river and its flood plain.

Cross the gully above Quarry Pond (another legacy of the mining company) and turn left at the next crosspath to make your way to the coastguard station. In this area, the remains of arrows have been found. These were fashioned by groups hunting the woodland animals that had returned as the climate improved around 9500 BC. Continue to the top of Warren Hill to enjoy the view and look down over the Double Dykes, a defensive earthwork constructed by the Celtic Iron Age people about 100 BC to defend their flourishing settlement and port on the harbour side of the Head. During that time Hengistbury was one of Britain's most important trading ports, exchanging metals, slaves and hunting dogs for luxury goods from the Mediterranean including wine and purple glass which could be fashioned into jewellery.

Follow the path down Warren Hill for just a few yards and take the first narrow path on the right. This leads back along the eastern side of Hengistbury Head through old woods and by the side of ponds covered with lilies. In front of Quarry Pond, turn left at the crosstrack to bear right round the pond. Go up the steps ahead and at the crosstrack turn left for a few yards, then right to walk back over the heath to the tip of the headland. Retrace your steps downhill to the ferry landing.

You can take the ferry for a leisurely harbour trip back to Christchurch Town Quay. Turn right from the landing on Christchurch Quay, past Place Mill, then left following the sign to the Tricycle Museum into the car park.

## Historical Notes

**Christchurch Priory:** When the Saxons established their settlement between the Avon and the Stour, they called their new town 'Tweoxneam', later Twynham – 'the place between the waters'. The name was, of course, eminently suitable but a legend explains why this was changed to Christchurch. Evidently, the Saxons wished to build their church on St Catherine's Hill, over a mile north of the town. Materials were assembled there but each night they were mysteriously removed to the present site of the Priory. Eventually the workmen accepted the new site in the heart of the town and began building. Unfortunately one of the roof beams was too short and the workmen went home for the night. In the morning it was found to be the right length and fitted perfectly. The astonished builders recollected that there had been an extra workman among their number who did not appear at mealtimes and never collected his pay. They believed this must have been the divine carpenter, Christ, and so the town was renamed Christchurch.

The 'miraculous beam' can be seen today over the arch at the south side of the Lady Chapel inside the Priory established by the Normans on the site of the Saxon church. The Priory contains so much that is beautiful that it is only possible to mention a few features here, among them the magnificent Norman nave flanked by semi-circular arches resting on massive pillars, and the 14th century quire screen. The lower half of the screen has pedestals carved with different kinds of foliage and little animals around the niches. Also dating from the 14th century is the reredos behind the High Altar which has told the whole Christmas story in carved stone to generations of worshippers who could not read.

**The Red House Museum:** The oldest part of this building dates from the 18th century and was a workhouse for the 'comfortable support of the numerous poor of the parish of Christchurch'. Christchurch was never a rich town, deriving its income at that time chiefly from fishing and smuggling. The museum includes among its many fine displays a gallery of costume and an art gallery. Within the grounds is a walled herb garden.
Opening times: Tuesday to Saturday 10 am to 5 pm. Sunday 2 pm to 5 pm. Bank Holiday Mondays 10 am to 5 pm.

**Christchurch Tricycle Museum:** Housed in two restored monastery buildings this is a unique collection of early, mainly Victorian, tricycles. It is open daily June to September 10 am to 5.30 pm, and weekends only Easter, April, May and October.

**Stanpit Marsh:** This nature reserve is a surprisingly remote wildlife area of almost 150 acres. There are both salt and freshwater marshes, sandy banks, gravel beds, scrublands and large stands of reeds providing the right conditions for a wide variety of birdlife and plants. A leaflet containing a map and details of the marsh's wildlife is available. For this, and all information about Christchurch, contact the Information Office in the High Street, Tel: 0202 471780.

**Hengistbury Head:** The site is recognised internationally for the importance of its prehistoric remains and is scheduled as an ancient monument. It is also famous for its wildlife, especially dragonflies and migrating birds. Several excellent booklets are available, including a detailed and colourful guide to Hengistbury Head Nature Trail. These can be obtained at the information centre near Double Dykes next to the Ranger's Office. Children will enjoy a ride in the land train which runs from Double Dykes to the ferry landing.

# The smugglers' coast – around Barton on Sea

## (Solent Way – Mudeford Quay to Taddiford Gap)

**Introduction:** From Mudeford Quay the Solent Way follows the coastline of Christchurch Bay to Milford on Sea and Hurst Spit. Housing developments spread inland for almost the whole way but there remains a delightful area where paths still lead over open countryside to the sea. This circular walk follows smugglers' tracks as it explores a countryside almost as remote today as it was during the 18th and 19th centuries when the freetraders landed their illicit cargoes at convenient inlets on the coast. These narrow valleys carved by small chalk streams flowing into the sea are known locally as 'bunnies'.

   This is a walk to be taken slowly as there is a great deal to enjoy on the way. The route runs east along the coast from Barton on Sea, a small resort famous for the fossils found in the soft clay of its cliffs. All the way there are spectacular views over the whole sweep of Christchurch Bay and to the hills of the Isle of Wight. And it is a walk full of contrasts. Just past Becton Bunny the route turns inland to explore a quiet countryside of old oak woods, narrow lanes and heathland paths. And there is a most conveniently sited pub at the halfway point.

**Distance:** Mudeford Quay to Taddiford Gap on the Solent Way 5 miles. Circular walk 4 miles. OS Landranger series 1:50 000 map 195 Bournemouth, Purbeck and surrounding area or OS Leisure series 1:25 000 map 22 New Forest.

**Refreshments:** In Barton on Sea there are the Ventana pub, the Beachcomber Café, and Sun Cottage for afternoon tea. Halfway round the circular walk, at Downton, the Royal Oak pub serves meals throughout the day and has a playground for children.

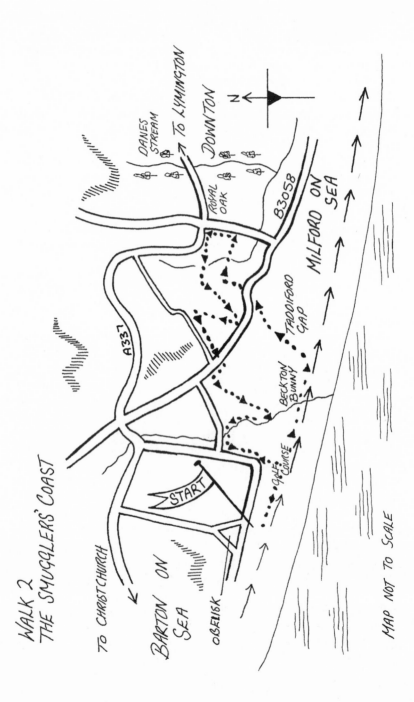

WALK 2
THE SMUGGLERS' COAST

TO CHRISTCHURCH

BARTON ON SEA

OBELISK

START

A337

DANES STREAM

TO LYMINGTON

DOWNTON

ROYAL OAK

B3058

MILFORD ON SEA

TADDIFORD GAP

BECKTON BUNNY

GOLF COURSE

N

MAP NOT TO SCALE

**How to get there:** The walk starts from the car park on the sea front at Barton on Sea, about 6 miles west of Lymington. Approaching along the A337 from Lymington, cross the B3058 and continue in the direction of Christchurch. Ignore the first turning signposted to Barton on Sea and turn left following the second signposted road. This runs due south to the sea front. Turn left in front of the obelisk on the front, then almost immediately right into the car park (parking charges, except October to March). There are Wilts and Dorset buses to the sea front from Lymington and Bournemouth and also from New Milton. Ring 0202 673555 for details.

**Solent Way – Mudeford Quay to Taddiford Gap:** From the quay walk back beside the car park and follow the sea front promenade ahead. On the left you pass Gundimore, a cream-coloured house, built to resemble a Persian tent in 1796 for the MP William Stuart Rose. Among his visitors were the romantic writers Coleridge and Southey and Sir Walter Scott, who wrote part of *Marmion* during his stay.

Follow the sea front past the beach huts at Avon Beach and continue past the next row of huts beneath Friars Cliff. The esplanade continues but I suggest you make a short diversion to visit the lovely woodlands around Steamer Point. Just before the last of the beach huts, turn left up the cliff, then half right to follow the clifftop to the Information and Display Centre beside the gates into the woodlands, close to the Coastguard Training School. Follow the path into the woods for a short distance, then turn left and keep to the path as it curves back to a picnic area on the clifftop with magnificent views. From there, flights of wooden steps lead down the cliff. Turn left and walk along the beach. On the top of the cliffs on your left are the gardens of Highcliffe Castle which can also be visited.

The Walkford Brook runs into the sea down an attractive wooded valley, called Chewton Bunny. Turn left and follow the footpath beside the scrub-covered cliff to walk through the trees with the brook on your right. When the path ceases, turn left up some steps and continue along the side of the valley, following a lane past the Mill House and the footpath sign just beyond. Turn right along the main Christchurch Road, the A337, and follow it as far as Western Avenue. Bear right and follow the avenue back to the sea.

Turn left to walk along the clifftop to the car park close to the obelisk in Barton on Sea. Now follow the route of the circular walk as far as Taddiford Gap, then turn to Walk Three.

**The Walk:** From the car park on Barton sea front turn left to follow the Solent Way over the wide green lawns fringing the low cliffs on your right. Take care not to go too close to the edge as these soft cliffs are very unstable. Rain seeping through the top layers of gravel weakens the clay beneath causing it to 'slump' or slip and unlike the Solent coastline further east these cliffs are exposed to the full force of waves whipped up by south-westerly gales. They are vanishing into the sea at the rate of one metre a year. Sea-swept boulders now protect the foreshore in an attempt to halt this process. Embedded in the clay are fossils dating back 45 million years. There are dazzling views of Christchurch Bay sheltered to the west by the dark cliffs of Hengistbury Head and to the east by the low shingle bank of Hurst Spit with its gleaming white lighthouse. Across the water is the curve of the Isle of Wight's Tennyson Down and the Needles sharply outlined against the sky.

The houses over the green on the left cease abruptly at the entrance to the golf course on Barton Common. Keep straight on through a small gate and continue along the clifftop with the golf course on the left. In just under ½ mile the path dips at the approach to Beckton Bunny. Turn left to cross a bridge over the steep-sided inlet, then bear right to keep on along the clifftop. The wire fence of Becton Farm is close on the left. The path dips downhill towards the beach at the foot of Taddiford Gap, another bunny used by smugglers in times past ('taddi' is a local word for a toad). Now the inlet is almost choked by fallen cliffs and blocks of concrete which formed part of the coastal defences during the last war.

A footpath sign points left indicating a path leading inland up the shallow valley along the smugglers' route. Leave the Solent Way and follow the path as it rises gently towards a distant line of woodland. Over the fields to the right is Hordle House, now a school, near the site of Hordle church demolished in 1830 and rebuilt two miles inland. The old village of Hordle, mentioned in the Domesday Book, with its salt pans, has long since vanished into the sea.

The path crosses a car park to a road, the B3058. Over the road, a few yards to the right, a footpath sign points left. Climb the stile and take the footpath over a field, with a deep ditch on your right, towards the woods ahead. Climb the next stile and cross a concrete bridge over the Danes Stream. Now a little path climbs gently up the slope ahead into the shade of an old oak wood. Growing close to the sea, the oaks are short and twisted into fantastic shapes, their upper branches carved by the prevailing south-westerly wind. The path bears left to follow the edge of the wood, then right over the fields to meet a lane in Downton. Follow the lane left beneath a canopy of pine trees to the main road, the A337. On the corner stands the Royal Oak, a charming black and white country pub with tiny arched porches and a tree that apparently grows out of the wall.

Turn left along the wide verge of the road for a few yards to a footpath sign pointing over the field on your left. Follow the sign straight over the field to enter the trees at the start of a beautiful path winding through a jungle of ancient oak and ash trees. Their cracked and creviced branches provide food and homes for tree creepers and woodpeckers and shelter for woodland plants, bluebells, windflowers and ferns. The path crosses the Danes Stream again over a rustic bridge, tunnels beneath arches of rhododendrons and climbs a little to enter a very different wood with open glades beneath Scots pines.

Go straight over a crosstrack to leave the wood and approach the B3058. Just before the road look carefully for a footpath sign on your right. Turn right and follow the direction of the sign over a field. Cross the stile and continue towards a small red-brick house, Angels Cottage. Cross the stile beside the house and with the cottage on your left join Angel Lane. Turn left along this narrow, oak-shaded lane to the B3058. Bear right here for about 100 yards and cross the road to where a gravel track runs beside the road. Look carefully over the gravel on your left for a footpath sign, rather obscured by trees. Follow the sign, left, through woodland with Barton Common through the trees on your right. The path can be muddy in places but soon rises to cross more open land with the golf course on your left. The path dips over the common with the sea ahead to join a crossing track.

Bear right and follow this attractive path which leads over the common and through woods. The path crosses a stream, flowing into Beckton Bunny, by means of a bridge constructed of railway sleepers still showing the grooves made by the shoes which held the lines. When the way meets a road, turn left to return to the clifftop. Retrace your steps, right, along the cliffs to the car park on Barton sea front.

## Historical Notes

**Barton on Sea:** Barton is a very old settlement, mentioned as being 'in the New Forest' in the Domesday Book. Axe heads dating from the Old Stone Age have been found on the common and can be seen in the Ashmolean Museum in Oxford. Celtic pottery has also been found nearby. Very little of old Barton remains today owing to the constant erosion of the cliffs. Cliff Terrace, now a small group of shops, was originally Barton Court Hotel. During the First World War it was used as a convalescent home for British troops. Indian troops who fought in Europe during the First War were also sent to Barton to convalesce and the obelisk close to the sea front commemorates their stay. Barton is still involved in world events. In 1956 Barton House, on the sea front overlooking Christchurch Bay, was taken over by the British Council for Aid to Refugees. Many came from the countries of Eastern Europe and an Orthodox chapel was built for them in the grounds.

But the soft clay cliffs which spelt disaster for so many of Barton's residents have yielded up fossils known to be 45 million years old and as a result the Barton Cliffs have been designated a Site of Special Scientific Interest. The fossils are the remains of sea creatures including alligators, crocodiles, sharks and giant snakes. They flourished beneath a sun hotter than that of the tropics, in the warm, shallow seas which at that time flooded the chalk of the Hampshire Basin and deposited the clay which today crumbles to reveal their bones.

**Chewton Bunny (Solent Way), Beckton Bunny and Taddiford Gap:** Until quite recent times, smuggling, particularly of tea and tobacco, and wines, spirits, silks and laces from France, was a flourishing local industry along the south coast. The wild countryside of the New Forest held many hiding places for goods destined for Burley, Ringwood, Fordingbridge or Salisbury, and these inlets into the low Barton cliffs with commanding views of

Christchurch Bay made ideal landing places. The whole activity was carefully organised. Capital was invested in a shipload of dutiable goods across the Channel by those with a little cash to spare, perhaps the local squire or a wealthy farmer. Help in manning craft, unloading the goods on to the backs of ponies often 'borrowed' from farms for the night, and leading them to the safety of the Forest villages, was readily available at a time when a labourer's wage averaged about seven shillings a week. 'Runs' were often planned in inns where men would talk as casually about 'Jim the smuggler' as they would about 'Jack the grocer'. To capture the flavour of the times read Thomas Hardy's short story *The Distracted Preacher.*

**Danes Stream:** The name of this small stream owes its origin to a legend. It is said that when the Danes landed on this coast they fought a fierce battle with the Saxons at Wootton Rough just over the present border of the New Forest close to the source of the stream. There is an old belief that every year on the anniversary of the battle the water in the stream turns red.

**Steamer Point Woodland and Highcliffe Castle (Solent Way):** The woodlands at Steamer Point formed part of the grounds of the now ruined Highcliffe Castle and were originally landscaped by 'Capability' Brown. A welcoming Information and Display Centre provides an excellent introduction to the area's varied wildlife. The warden runs a once-monthly children's Nature Watch Group and guided walks by prior arrangement. Ring 0425 272479 for details.

Highcliffe Castle dates from 1835 and was built for Lord Stuart de Rothesay who entertained many royal visitors here. The castle suffered two fires and is not open to the public. However, the surrounding gardens are open and there is access to the beach.

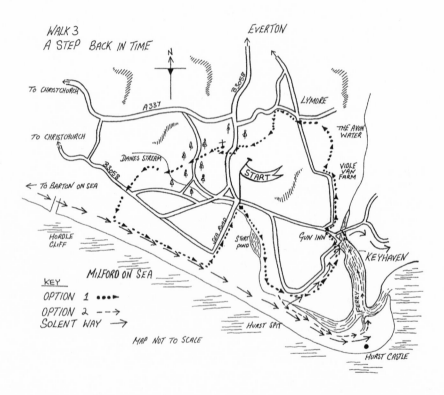

WALK 3
A STEP BACK IN TIME

EVERTON

N

TO CHRISTCHURCH

A337

TO CHRISTCHURCH

B3058

LYMORE

THE AVON WATER

DANES STREAM

B3058

VIDLE VAN FARM

START

← TO BARTON ON SEA

SEA ROAD

STURT POND

GUN INN

KEYHAVEN

HORDLE CLIFF

MILFORD ON SEA

FERRY

KEY
OPTION 1 ••••►
OPTION 2 ‐‐→
SOLENT WAY →

HURST SPIT

MAP NOT TO SCALE

HURST CASTLE

# A step back in time – around Milford on Sea, Hurst Castle Spit and Keyhaven

## (Solent Way – Taddiford Gap to Keyhaven)

**Introduction:** This circular walk explores an area of Outstanding Natural Beauty where time seems to stand still. As you follow paths over bird-haunted marshes to a tiny village tucked away down narrow lanes, half-hidden by trees, 20th century noise and bustle belongs to a different planet!

The walk starts from the centre of Milford on Sea, a delightfully homely resort which preserves the atmosphere of a village with its small green overlooked by the stubby spire of a Norman church. Marshland paths lead to the beginning of Hurst Spit where the walk joins the Solent Way. Here there is a choice of routes, and I will give details of both. In summer, I suggest a walk along the Spit to visit Hurst Castle followed by a ferry ride to Keyhaven to continue the walk. In winter, when the ferry is not running, you may prefer to avoid the need to walk back along the Spit and follow the sea wall to Keyhaven instead. There are splendid views from both routes of the Spit, the shipping in the Solent, and the Isle of Wight from Yarmouth to the Needles.

At Keyhaven, the walk leaves the Solent Way to discover a completely different countryside of woods and streams before returning to Milford along the clifftop. Here, too, there is a dramatic change of scenery as the cliffs of Christchurch Bay, overlooking sand and shingle beaches scalloped by the waves, give way to mud flats and saltmarsh penned by sea walls.

**Distance:** Taddiford Gap to Keyhaven on the Solent Way (short route) 4.5 miles. Via Hurst Spit and ferry 5.5 miles. Circular walk

5.5 miles (short route). Via Hurst Spit and ferry to Keyhaven 6.5 miles. The Spit is hard, stony walking so allow extra time. As you may also like time to visit the castle, I would recommend taking a whole day for the longer walk. Tracing the route on the OS Landranger series 1:50 000 is complicated as you need both map 195 Bournemouth, Purbeck and surrounding area and map 196 The Solent. It is better to use map 22 in the Outdoor Leisure series.

**Refreshments:** Milford on Sea provides all facilities including three historic pubs, the Red Lion, the Smugglers Inn and the White Horse Inn. There are cafés on Milford sea front. The café in Hurst Castle is open during the summer months. The Gun Inn at Keyhaven also serves meals.

**How to get there:** The walk starts in the centre of Milford on Sea, from the car park in Sea Road close to its junction with the High Street. Approaching Milford along the A337 turn south in Everton along the B3058. In a little over a mile be ready to turn sharp left in front of Milford Green following the sign for the beach, Keyhaven and car park. Cross straight over the High Street into Sea Road and after a few yards turn left into the car park.

Milford is served by Wilts and Dorset buses from Lymington, Ringwood, Salisbury and Bournemouth. Ring 0202 673555 for details.

**Keyhaven ferry:** The Hurst Castle ferry operates daily from May to the end of October and during the Easter holidays. Ferries depart from Keyhaven on the hour from 10 am and return from Hurst Castle on the half-hour until 5.30 pm. Extra services are sometimes run at winter weekends and Bank Holidays depending on the weather. Ring New Milton (0425) 610784 for details. The trip to the castle takes about half an hour.

**Hurst Castle:** The castle is open weekends only from 1st October to 31st March, 10 am to 4 pm. The rest of the year it is open daily 10 am to 6 pm.

**Solent Way – Taddiford Gap to Keyhaven (Gun Inn):** Climb to the top of Hordle Cliff from the Gap to follow the clear path ahead along the clifftop towards Milford on Sea. These higher cliffs were used by smugglers as a look-out. They also made a good vantage point during the Second World War and are still littered with the remains of concrete gun emplacements. There is a splendid view of the cliffs of West Wight and the coloured sands of Alum Bay.

Ahead you will see Hurst Spit and the recent housing developments spreading west from Milford on Sea. The path becomes gravelled as you approach the village and the cliffs slope gently down towards a rather sinister looking grey building on the sea front. Continue, leaving the building on your left. Keep on along the sea front passing the Marine café to follow the single bank with Sturt Pond on your left. As the pond narrows and is crossed by a bridge continue along the route of the Walk (see below) as far as Keyhaven (Gun Inn) and then turn to Walk Four.

**The Walk:** From the car park follow the narrow gravelled footpath running east along the south bank of the Danes Stream. Cross a small bridge and continue eastwards. Now, to your right, all trace of Milford disappears and wide reedbeds conceal the stream. Have binoculars ready as this is a birdwatcher's paradise. Reed and sedge warblers breed here gaining strength before their autumn migration, and herons poise their S-shaped necks motionless beside brackish pools. The reeds thin around a small lagoon, Sturt Pond. In winter especially, this is alive with birds. Waders include curlews probing deep into the water with their long, curved beaks, and oyster-catchers, conspicuous by their orange-red beaks, seeking their prey at a different level. Wigeon, recognised by their yellow-crowned chestnut heads, predominate among the ducks.

Cross the bridge at the point where the Danes Stream flows out of the lagoon and climb the shingle bank ahead to look out over the sea. Now there are wonderful views across the water to the Island and ahead along Hurst Spit to the castle. Here you join the **Solent Way**. Bear left along the shingle bank with the Danes Stream running parallel beside you. When you come to another bridge over the stream on the left, there is a choice of routes for the next part of the walk to Keyhaven.

**Option 1:** (Recommended May to October and winter weekends when the ferry runs from Keyhaven.) Do not cross the bridge but keep straight on along the rough shingle bank of Hurst Spit. Your reward is a marvellous view in all directions – west over the breaking waves of Christchurch Bay, east over Keyhaven Marshes, one of the finest bird sanctuaries on the south coast, and ahead to the downs of the Isle of Wight.

Very little grows on this great pebble bank but as you approach the castle, which is built upon a deposit of firm clay only lightly overlain with shingle, the ground is carpeted with flowers. Among them are cushions of pink-flowered thrift, tall seakale, their clustered flowerheads as much as a foot across, and delicate yellow horned poppies. In July, along the edges of the saltmarsh below the castle, blooms a Hurst Spit speciality, golden samphire.

The massive outer walls of the castle are additions made in Victorian times to a small fortress built by Henry VIII. As well as defence, the castle was also used as a prison. Charles I was held here before he was taken to London for trial and execution.

A unique feature of the Spit are the two working lighthouses: the red one within the castle walls and the conspicuous white one. When ships enter the Solent they must get these two lighthouses in line to avoid the shingle banks close to the Needles rocks.

Board the ferry at the small quay opposite the entrance to the castle and relax as the boat makes its winding way back to the jetty at Keyhaven.

**Option 2:** It is possible of course to walk both ways along the Spit but walking along the rough shingle for 3 miles can be exhausting. So you may prefer this route to Keyhaven. Bear left to descend the shingle, cross the wooden bridge and continue along the road ahead towards Keyhaven until a track joins on the right. Leave the road and take the track along the sea wall over mud flats and salt marsh, a marvellous habitat for birds including huge flocks of geese. The marshes echo with their calls. The sea wall leads to Keyhaven Harbour and the jetty. The ferry to Hurst Castle runs from here.

From the jetty the walk takes one route again beside this attractive little harbour dotted with fishing boats, sailing yachts and dinghies. Follow the road left in front of the Keyhaven Yacht Club then right towards the Gun Inn, draped with fishing nets and lobster pots, and, as you might expect, complete with a small cannon mounted above the porch.

The walk now leaves the Solent Way which turns right in Keyhaven over the Avon Water. Keep straight on, following the footpath beside the road, past the Gun Inn and Hawker's Cottage to a small triangle of grass. Bear right before the grass to Lymore Lane, then right again for only a few yards to a lane on your left. Follow this in the direction of Vidle Van farm, passing some picturesque cottages deep-thatched with buttressed walls. Leave the road and turn right following the footpath sign to Lymore. At a crosstrack follow the clear line of the path ahead.

Now there is the first hint of the remote cluster of houses hidden in woodland which is Lymore village. The path dips to a stile leading to a narrow lane, thickly hedged with oaks and hawthorn, in front of a long, low thatched house. Turn left and follow the lane as it winds beside tiny streams and through copses of tangled willows and oak trees. Houses, gardens and orchards blend quite naturally with this woodland setting.

To continue the walk, take the first lane on the left to Lymore Lane. Bear right, then almost immediately left down School Lane. Follow the footpath sign on your left for Milford. This leads through woodland and then bears a little right beside a field with the woods on your right. When the path leaves the edge of the woods, keep straight on across a field – you will see the small spire of Milford church to the right. The path bears a little right over the next field towards houses and the spire is now to the left.

When the path reaches the main road, the B3058, turn left along the pavement, passing the red-brick walls of the early 18th century Old Vicarage. Just before a road on the right leads to the church, go through a small white gate to cross the churchyard. Milford's partly Norman church is well worth a visit. From the south porch walk round the tower to a crosspath. Turn left to leave the churchyard through a white kissing-gate which leads, appropriately, to Love Lane.

Follow this pleasant path sunk between mossy banks straight over a crossing road. At the next crossing look over the road to the right to where the footpath continues steeply downhill to a bridge over the Danes Stream. As you cross the bridge look through the trees for a glimpse of the old mill which dates from 1760 but is on the site of a much older building. The last miller, Mr Stone, finished his work here in 1899.

Bear right along the wooded valley beside the Danes Stream. Cross a road and continue with the stream still on your right. The path goes over a footbridge and the stream now flows to your left. At a crosspath, bear left, then left again to another bridge. After the bridge leave the streamside and continue up Woodland Way towards the coast. Cross the road ahead and follow De La Warr road as it makes its way over several minor roads to the clifftop. Bear left along the cliffs towards Milford. (This route follows the Solent Way.) At the Beach Café (the Needles Eye Café on the other side) turn left to cross the road and walk up Sea Road back to the centre of Milford and the car park on the right.

**Historical Notes**

**Milford on Sea:** Milford has the lively, welcoming atmosphere of a much loved village. Cliff erosion gave Milford a sea front in the late 18th century and in spite of the attempts of the local landlord, Colonel William Cornwallis-West, to turn this former inland parish into a seaside resort, Milford retained its quiet dignity, having little to do with the world of funfairs and candyfloss. The High Street is a pleasing mix of small shops, old inns and colour-washed cottages with curved Georgian bay windows.

All Saints church, dating from the middle of the 12th century, was built on the site of a Saxon church erected by Aelfric, who held the land, in about 1080. Of the Norman church only two round-headed arches on thick pillars with carved capitals and two doorways in the gable ends of the transepts survive. There is much to see but do not miss the small stained glass panel in the north-west window of the chancel which shows Charles I with a halo and holding a martyr's palm. No prizes for guessing which side the vicar was on!

The early 13th century tower with its narrow lancet windows and carved corbels under the eaves has most unusual lean-tos on either side. Perhaps they were built to shelter the monks from Christchurch who held services here or to accommodate the large numbers of workers in the local salt industry.

Nearby is Milford's village green, a remnant of a medieval common. It is a busy place today as the site for the village fête, a carnival and a Great Pumpkin Competition.

**Milford and Hordle Cliffs:** From these cliffs a ledge containing nodules of ironstone runs out to sea for nearly 2 miles. Until the beginning of this century a fleet of 30 or 40 boats would be at sea dredging for them as they were used in the manufacture of a cement that set readily under water, similar to that brought from Rome. Pieces washed up on the beach were eagerly collected by the local people and taken to Sowley pond near Beaulieu to be smelted. A track from the beach in Milford is still called the Mineway.

**Keyhaven**: The name of this small cluster of houses at the head of a narrow channel of navigable water known as Keyhaven Lake is derived from the Saxon 'cy-haefenn', cow-harbour, so there must have been a settlement here from earliest times. Among the fishing boats are many pleasure craft belonging to the Keyhaven Yacht Club and the Hurst Castle Sailing Club.

Hawker's Cottage, beside the Gun Inn, was the home of Colonel Peter Hawker who kept a diary for 52 years detailing his wildfowling exploits on the nearby marshes. Although a somewhat bloodthirsty account, his journals are an invaluable wildlife record. He also composed music and patented an improvement in the construction of the piano. A narrow channel in the harbour, Hawker's Lake, is called after him.

**Hurst Spit:** This great pebble bank has been built up by centuries of longshore drifting. Much less striking examples can be found along the whole of the Solent coastline. Protection of the coast to the west reduced the height of the Spit resulting in a serious breach in 1989. Since then New Forest District Council has deposited rubble to add two metres to the Spit's height and double its width, and between five and ten thousand tons of shingle are stored close by ready for emergencies.

**Hurst Castle:** The Tudor fortress built with stone from the ruins of Beaulieu Abbey was one of several designed to guard the Solent from possible French and Spanish attack. The central, twelve-sided tower has two floors and a basement and is surrounded by a curtain wall on which there are three semicircular bastions. Charles I was, as Sir Thomas Herbert put it, 'slenderly accommodated' here for 19 days in 1648. Another prisoner was Father Paul Atkinson, a

Franciscan, arrested for Roman Catholic activity in 1700 and held until his death 29 years later. His ghost is said to haunt the old tower.

During Victorian times many additions were made to the castle including two large wings to the east and west. The castle remained fortified through to the end of the Second World War when anti-aircraft and searchlight batteries were situated close by.

# Wildlife magic – Keyhaven, Pennington and Oxey marshes

(Solent Way – Keyhaven to Moses Dock)

**Introduction:** The vast expanse of marshland between Keyhaven and Lymington is a spectacular wildlife reserve. The best way to explore this remote area is to follow the sea wall which runs the whole way to Lymington. This is the route of the Solent Way and forms the first 3 miles of the circular walk.

Seaward of the wall great numbers of birds, including many rare species such as ruffs, follow the ebb tide probing the mud and saltmarsh for worms and shellfish. Offshore, little terns nest on the shingle banks. Inland, the low-lying brackish lagoons and rough pasture originally reclaimed for farming purposes and the salt industry provide homes and food for many other, perhaps more usual birds, including herons and swans. Kestrels and sparrowhawks scan the grassland and in summer skylarks and meadow pipits sing overhead.

Today it is hard to imagine that for 700 years until the early 19th century these tranquil marshes were the scene of an important industry, the production of sea salt. From the sea wall the extensive remains of former salterns – embanked enclosures, windpump mounds, even some buildings – are clearly visible.

The walk leaves the Solent Way to follow field paths past historic houses and inns, and takes a final look at the Avon Water on its way back to Keyhaven.

**Distance:** Keyhaven to Moses Dock on the Solent Way 3 miles. Circular walk 5 miles. OS Landranger series 1:50 000 map 196 The Solent. OS Outdoor Leisure series 1:25 000 map 22 New Forest.

**Refreshments:** The Gun Inn, Keyhaven. The Chequers Inn, Lower Pennington (circular walk only).

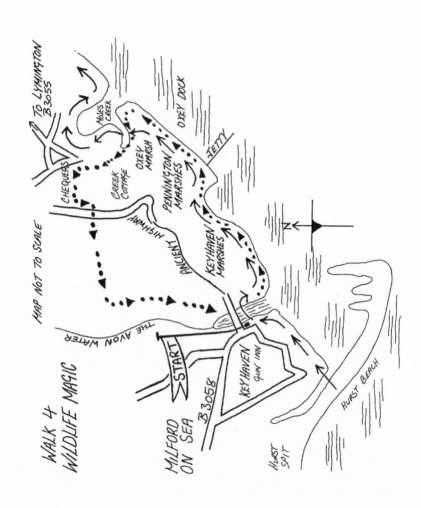

WALK 4
WILDLIFE MAGIC

MAP NOT TO SCALE

TO LYMINGTON
B3055

MOSES CREEK

OXEY DOCK

JETTY

OXEY MARSH

PENNINGTON MARSHES

CREEK COTTAGE

CHEQUERS

KEYHAVEN MARSHES

ANCIENT HIGHWAY

THE AVON WATER

N

START

B3058

MILFORD ON SEA

KEYHAVEN
GUN INN

HURST BEACH

HURST SPIT

**How to get there:** The best approach to Keyhaven is via Milford on Sea. Approaching Milford along the A337 turn south in Everton along the B3058 following the sign for Milford and Keyhaven. In a little over a mile be ready to turn sharply left following the sign for Keyhaven. Turn sharp left again in a few yards when you meet the High Street and follow the lane to Keyhaven. Turn left and park in the car park on your right opposite the Gun Inn.

There is no public transport to Keyhaven, but Milford, which is well served by buses, is only a mile away and can be reached by a pleasant walk along the sea front.

**Solent Way – Keyhaven to Moses Dock:** Follow the route of Walk Four from Keyhaven along the sea wall as far as Moses Dock, then turn to Walk Five.

**The Walk:** The car park in Keyhaven is opposite the Gun Inn. With the inn on your left, walk down the lane immediately on your right. Harbour sights and sounds greet you as you cross the sluice gates over the Avon Water and look seawards over Keyhaven Lake. Gulls screech overheard, busy little turnstones scamper along the water's edge, tipping the pebbles over with their beaks, and cormorants stand stiffly on the boats, spreading out their large black wings to dry.

A footpath sign on the right invites you to follow the sea wall. Very soon all trace of habitation has vanished and vast marshes forming a paradise for huge numbers of birds spread on either side. Have binoculars ready as apart from the birds you may expect to see – curlews, dunlins, redshanks and oyster-catchers – you should see Sandwich terns with their forked tails, striking black and white markings and graceful swooping flight and perhaps a rarity such as an avocet, recognised by its pencil-thin upturned beak.

The wall skirts a pool on the left to continue past the remains of former salterns. From the wall you can see the embanked enclosures which held the sea water as it evaporated in the sun. You can also see occasional mounds that supported the windpumps which forced the concentrated brine into coal-fed boiling houses.

Follow the wall through this remote watery world past a jetty where fishermen dig for bait. Just beyond lie shingle banks which are the carefully protected nesting sites of the rare little tern, only recently arrived on our shores, This small bird is a delight to watch as it hovers over tidal creeks, slender wings arching above its snowy back, before diving to catch a tiny fish in its black-tipped yellow beak.

To the left of the recently reconstructed sea wall there is a small promontory laid with large stones. Formerly there was an inlet here and the stones of the 14th century Oxey Dock, where coal barges unloaded, have been replaced through the efforts of the Friends of Lymington Museum. The National Rivers Authority provided the labour and Hampshire County Council the funds.

The path skirts Oxey Marsh to follow the left bank of an inlet, the entrance to Moses Dock, another former unloading depot for coal barges. On the right you come to a bridge beside a sluice gate leading to part of the sea wall. Here the walk leaves the Solent Way. Do not cross the bridge but continue straight on, down some steps, beside the inlet. Soon you will see Creek Cottage at the head of the old dock. Turn left at the stile in front of the house and walk to a minor road. Bear right here to follow the road past Chequers Green with the Chequers Inn just beyond.

Follow the footpath sign pointing left beside the green. Cross a stile to take a very narrow footpath which leads over another stile into a meadow. From here there is a good view of 18th century Pennington House. After a few yards turn right over a stile and then bear left again to cross fields and stiles and pass a flooded quarry – much appreciated by coots and moorhens – to a lane. The route now skirts the entrance to a tip and fringes some gravel extraction works, but you are soon past them. Cross the lane and follow the footpath sign straight ahead. The path bears a little left (the works have slightly altered the angle of the path as shown on the OS maps) then continues south. At first the track lies beside the gravel extraction works but it soon becomes a pleasant green way bordered by gorse and hawthorn thickets. It joins the Old Highway, a narrow road that used to link Lower Pennington with Keyhaven and must have been used extensively in the past. Bear right at the side of the thick reed beds, which almost conceal the Avon Water. Swallows roost here and shy reed buntings – the males have black heads with a white collar – may be glimpsed feeding on the seeds of the marsh plants. Cross the sluice gates again to return to the car park opposite the Gun Inn.

## Historical Notes

**The nature of the coastal marshes:** Although the great wealth of birdlife is the most striking feature of the marshes, such variety would not exist without the ingenuity of plants. Salt is generally toxic to plants but some, notably glasswort with its upright stems surrounded by fleshy spikes, and cordgrass – spartina – are specially adapted to thrive in the mud, holding it together to form saltmarsh. Spartina has special glands to dispose of salt, thick leathery leaves to resist the tides and two root systems, a mat of surface roots and deep tap roots, with air channels, to hold it firm.

Once these 'pioneers' have taken hold, gradually raising the level of the mud, other plants such as sea purslane, sea lavender and sea spurrey can invade. Plant debris provides food for the tiny organisms feeding the hordes of worms and shellfish which in their turn attract the birds. A type of spartina which did not encourage the growth of other plants has spread extensively but for some reason, not fully explained, it is dying back, exposing the mud.

**Salterns:** The salt trade flourished in this area for 700 years. In 1743 a long row of 163 salterns ran along the Solent shore from Pylewell, just east of Lymington, west to Hurst Spit. The WI publication *It Happened in Hampshire* quotes from a guide book written about 1800 which describes the salt making process:

> The seawater is just pumped into pans, which are shallow square pits, dug in the earth. In these it is exposed to the heat of the sun, till so much of its freshness is evaporated, as to leave it seven times stronger than it was in its natural state. It is next pumped into flat iron pans, eight or ten feet square and as many inches deep. In these the brine is boiled over a fierce fire, till nothing is left but pure salt. This, being drained a proper time, in convenient vessels, is fit for use.

The average boiling season lasted 16 weeks, each pan producing some 3 tons of salt a week. The ships that docked in the inlets and waterways across the marshes brought coal to fire the boiling houses and sailed with cargoes of salt. Most was for home consumption, especially vital for the preservation of food for the fleet at Portsmouth. Overseas destinations included North America, Newfoundland, Holland and the Baltic.

The government had always exacted a heavy tax from the salt producers and by the 1840s increased taxation meant that the industry could no longer compete with the mining of rock salt in the north-west, now brought cheaply southwards by rail. This great industry of the Solent shore died with the closure of the last boiling house in 1865.

**Creek Cottage:** This mainly Victorian house built of mellow brick stands at the head of Moses Dock, an inlet which must have been the scene of great activity when the salt industry flourished here. You will see two Tudor barns close by. The one closer to the water was possibly a boiling house and the other was probably used for storing the salt.

**The Chequers Inn:** An old inn which derives its name from 'Exchequer' as it was the house where the saltworkers' wages were kept.

The inn is partly constructed from the timbers of a French fishing boat *Le Hareng Rouge*. In the past many local families earned their living fishing for the winkles, which were plentiful in the Solent. But towards the end of the 19th century most of the winkles were harvested by the French who had their own method of fishing. They would hang rush mats over the sides of the ship then blow a whistle, which had the same effect on the winkles as the music of the Pied Piper had on the children of Hamelin. Hypnotised, the winkles climbed up the mats into the waiting hands of the fishermen. Every year, millions of winkles migrated west, and the crew of *Le Hareng Rouge*, misled by an earlier than usual migration, blew their whistle in the midst of one of them. Millions of winkles climbed up the mats so quickly that the crew could not beat them off. The winkles filled the boat, which eventually sank with all on board. After a story like that, what French fisherman would dare pursue a winkle?

**Pennington House:** An early 18th century mansion standing in parkland framed by trees. In 1901, the Marquess of Headfort married Rosie Boote who was starring in *The Messenger Boy* at the

Gaiety Theatre. As they needed to retire from London society while everyone got used to the idea, they accepted the offer made by their friends, the Cornwallis-Wests, who lived at Newlands, close to Milford on Sea, to spend some time at this remote house.

The name Pennington means 'a settlement paying a penny rate'.

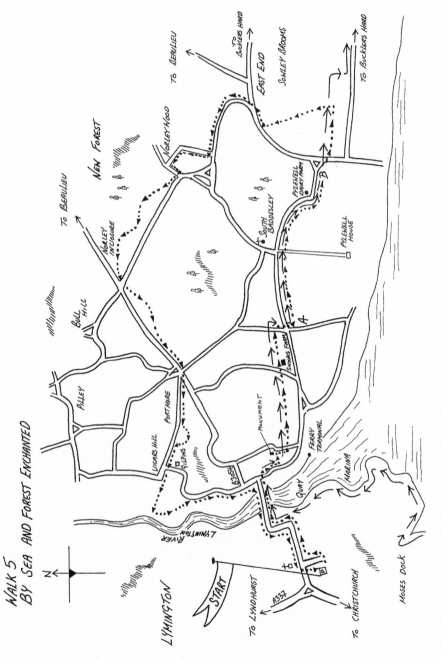

WALK 5
BY SEA AND FOREST ENCHANTED

MAP NOT TO SCALE

# 'By sea and forest enchanted' – Lymington and the southern New Forest

## (Solent Way – Moses Dock to Sowley Brooms crosstrack)

**Introduction:** The phrase 'by sea and forest enchanted', sometimes used to describe the historic port of Lymington, could not be more appropriate. For centuries the town has been associated with the sea and shipping, and once ships of up to 500 tons could berth by the cobbled quayside at the foot of the High Street. Today Lymington is as busy as ever with yachts and fishing boats, but it is also a vital part of New Forest life with a flourishing market dating from the 12th century. Settled comfortably at what was once the lowest fording point of the river as it flows between marshes into the Solent, and protected to the north by the unique medieval landscape of the New Forest, Lymington has a lovely setting matched by few other towns.

This walk explores part of Lymington and then goes further to look at some of the heaths and woodlands of the New Forest, declared a royal hunting forest in 1079 and still the property of the monarch. There is the promise of some magical moments – perhaps a glimpse of deer down a Forest ride or a family of dabchicks cruising among the reeds fringing the Lymington river.

The walker is free to ramble almost at will in the New Forest – the private areas such as the Beaulieu Manor Estate are well marked – so there is no need for footpath signs. However, this is not always an advantage. If the area is new to you, navigate carefully, pack a good supply of sustaining snacks and be prepared to tackle some muddy patches.

**Distance:** Moses Dock to Sowley Brooms crosstrack on the Solent

Way 5.5 miles. Circular walk 8.5 miles. OS Landranger series 1:50 000 The Solent. Also OS Outdoor Leisure series 1:25 000 map 22 New Forest.

**Refreshments:** Lymington has excellent pubs and teashops.

**How to get there:** The walk starts from a car park off St Thomas Street which is a continuation of the top end of the High Street in the centre of Lymington. Approaching from the north or west follow the signs for the Town Centre and the High Street. Drive down St Thomas Street for about 50 yards and follow a sign 'Toilets' to turn right down an entry just past Waitrose. The car park is divided into long- and short-stay sections. Approaching from the east, drive up the High Street, past the church on your right, and turn left following the car park sign.

After Easter, during the summer months, there is an information caravan in the car park.

If this car park is full, you will find others close by. Return to the High Street to start the walk. The car parks and High Street become crowded on market day, Saturday.

Lymington is well served by buses and trains. The walk passes the bus depot and the railway station.

**Solent Way – Moses Dock to Sowley Brooms crosstrack:** At the entrance to the inlet at Moses Dock, turn right over the bridge beside a sluice gate. Bear right along the sea wall and follow the wall as it makes its way towards Lymington around the former saltworks. The wall now runs to the right of Eight Acre Pond and round Normandy Farm Nature Reserve where the lattice pattern of the salt pans is clearly visible.

Ahead a forest of masts indicates the first of the marinas on the Lymington river where yachting is now of major importance. Go through the gate at the approach to the marina and follow the sea wall to a small dock. The route runs to the left of the marina office, so turn left for a few yards then right to a footpath sign. Turn right (the office is on your right) and walk to the sea wall to continue towards the Town Quay. You pass Lymington's fine sea water swimming pool, established in 1833 and an impressive building, originally the Bath House, now housing the Lymington Town Sailing

Club. Opposite is the Royal Lymington Yacht Club.

The Way beside the sea wall runs past a park then turns inland to take Quay Road. On the right is the Berthon Boat Co. named after the Revd Lyon Berthon, the designer of the famous collapsible lifeboat. He tested his designs at home by flooding the cellars of his Fareham vicarage! The black and white house projecting into the road is called, appropriately, Pressgang Cottage. Evidently it was formerly the Harlequin Inn, and the headquarters of the pressgang in 1800. The road leads to Lymington Town Quay. Walk past the quay to the foot of Quay Hill. Follow the route of Walk Five (see below) as far as Sowley Brooms crosstrack then turn to Walk Six.

**The Walk:** From the car park walk back to St Thomas Street, one of the oldest streets in Lymington, and turn right in the direction of the High Street. The mellow brick Monmouth House, built late in the 17th century takes its name from the group of Monmouth sympathisers, headed by the mayor, Thomas Dore, who met there in 1685.

Lymington parish church, dedicated to St Thomas, stands at the top of the wide High Street. The distinctive tower and cupola were added to a much older building of around 1250 by the town's inhabitants after the church was gutted by Puritan soldiers during the Civil War. As you walk down the High Street, past the bus depot, you will see the mix of elegant Georgian houses, bow-fronted cottages and little courts and alleyways which add so much to Lymington's charm.

Cross the road at the foot of the High Street and walk down cobbled Quay Hill which has the atmosphere of a fishing village. The quay is to the right but to continue the walk, turn left at the bottom of Quay Hill. **Solent Way walkers join here**. Follow Mill Lane and Waterloo Road, past the train station, and turn right over the level crossing. Continue across the Toll Bridge Dam. The dam, with two sluices, was built across the Lymington river by a merchant navy captain, William Cross, in 1731. He had acquired the rights to the mud flats from one Robert Pamplyn, Yeoman of the Robes to Charles I. Lymington residents were affected in two ways: their river was no longer navigable by large craft and Captain Cross insisted they paid a toll to cross his bridge. The toll was not abolished until 1968.

Turn right in the direction of the ferry and follow the waterside. The metal rails on the right cease, and opposite two gravel tracks lead left from the road. Turn left then almost immediately left again off the right-hand track, following the footpath sign. A woodland path leads uphill to an obelisk, raised in memory of Admiral Sir Harry Burrard Neale, who alone preserved the loyalty of his crew during the mutiny at the Nore.

Turn right down the lane just beyond the monument and take the first gravel track on your left. It may be marked by a house name, Halyards. Go through a small gate and now the path leads beside fields and through woods to a lane. Turn left for just a few yards, then right following the footpath sign past Snooks farm. When the gravel track meets a lane turn right to a minor road (to the point marked A on the map). At present the route of the Solent Way, which the walk is following, turns left along the minor road to follow it past the school at South Baddesley and bears left past Pylewell Dairy Farm. The route continues across the cattle grid, to the right of a grass triangle and over the stile into the field ahead indicated by a footpath sign (marked B on the map). A new route is planned for this section, so look for any new waymarking signs at A.

Once over the stile, you are within the official perambulation of the New Forest, but as this area is part of the privately owned Beaulieu Manor Estate, footpath signs mark rights of way as in other parts of the country.

The path becomes lovely now as it crosses fields and enters an old oak wood, Sowley Brooms. Soon you come to a crosstrack and here the walk leaves the Solent Way which continues straight on. Turn left along a path leading deeper into the woods. Among the quiet glades you may see deer and foxes, and many woodland birds such as woodpeckers and the little mouse-like tree creepers.

Leave the wood to cross a stile ahead and walk to another stile to your left. Bear a little left to cross more stiles and walk over the field ahead to a lane by a footpath sign. Turn right and follow the lane over East End bridge and up to a road junction. Turn left for Norleywood village. Now the real New Forest (outside the boundary of the Beaulieu Manor Estate) stretches northwards. There are over 100 square miles of Forest, administered by the Forestry Commission. Much of it is still a wilderness where you can wander freely and enjoy the richness of its unique wildlife.

Follow the road as it passes some isolated cob cottages and a pond covered with lilies and approaches the houses of the village. Opposite the first house, which is close to the road on your left, turn right down a gravel track. At a T-junction turn left to the road through Norleywood village. Bear right here and follow the road as it turns left. Leave the road and go through the gate on your right into Norley Inclosure, a large, very peaceful pinewood with a scattering of oaks and beeches.

After about 100 yards, leave the main track and bear left along a green path which wanders happily through the trees to bring you to a crosspath. Bear right for a short distance to another crosspath. Turn left to follow the woodland path to the western edge of Norley Inclosure where a gate leads to a car park.

Go through the gate and turn immediately left beside the Inclosure fence. Walk beside the fence to the minor road you followed earlier through Norleywood village. Cross over and take the heathland path ahead. When the path divides, bear right to come to the cattle grid across the B3054 on the Forest boundary. Just to the left of the grid you will see a path leading to a small footbridge. Take this way, and go through a gate to follow a very narrow path parallel with the road. The path meets the road past a small wooded area. Continue along the verge for about 80 yards to a signpost indicating several roads in Portmore. Bear right down Hundred Lane, signposted to Spinners Gardens. Follow this pleasant lane until you come to a footpath sign on your left leading into a pretty coppice wood, full of birdsong and wild flowers. If you do not mind a rather muddy path later and a few minutes longer walk, turn left into the wood and when you come to a stile, turn right to return to Hundred Lane. Or ignore the footpath sign and keep straight on.

Before you meet a lane, you pass a beautiful 18th century house on your left, called Gilpins. This was the home of William Gilpin, who became vicar of Boldre in 1777 and whose books, which included *Remarks on Forest Scenery* made such an impression on his contemporaries. He spent many hours in the forest studying the landscape, and his feeling for the 'picturesque' breathed new life into 18th century art.

Follow the bridleway sign over the lane and now from the top of Vicar's Hill there is a wide view over the valley of the Lymington river. The bridleway drops to Vicar's Hill farm and continues down a

49

rather steep slope beside the farm to the river bank. Turn left to follow the river towards Lymington. This is a beautiful – though possibly muddy – walk. The river winds lazily through dense thickets of reeds, bordered by wooded hillsides. Kingcups and yellow irises colour marshy areas, and bluebells encircle the tree roots and spill over on to the path.

The path winds through the trees to reach a minor road. Bear right to continue along the road and join your earlier route as you turn right over the Toll Bridge Dam in Lymington. Turning left down Waterloo Road retrace your route to Quay Hill. If you keep straight on at the foot of Quay Hill a charming cobbled way leads to the quay, where you might like to rest and enjoy the sights and sounds of the river before walking back up the High Street to your car.

## Historical Notes

**Lymington:** Celtic tribes were the first to settle in this area and built two forts. The later fort, possibly constructed about 500 BC, enclosed a seven-acre site just north of the present town. Known as Buckland Rings, it is still well preserved and has been protected from modern developers by strong local feeling.

Until the end of the 18th century Lymington flourished as a port noted for its foreign trade, as a producer of salt, and on the proceeds of what Daniel Defoe in 1720 termed 'rogueing and smuggling'. However in his *Literary Recollections* of 1776 the Reverend Richard Warner praises Lymington for its noteworthy 'moral and social beauty'. The town's many charming Georgian houses date from those prosperous days.

Today, Lymington once again bustles with life. A commercial fishing fleet operates out of the quay, two large marinas and river moorings attract yachts from around the world, and shipbuilding and repairing continues on both banks of the river. A regular ferry service runs from Lymington Pier to Yarmouth on the Isle of Wight.

Free guided walks around Lymington are run in the summer, usually on alternate Sunday afternoons and Wednesday evenings. For information ring Helen Theobald, 0590 644438 or Bill Klitz, 0590 679391.

The Buckland Trust has established a display telling the story of Buckland Rings in the old toll cottage, next to the Toll House Inn, north of the town beside the A337. Contact the landlord of the inn for information.

**Pylewell:** The mansion was the home of a Catholic family, the Welds. Notable members of the family included Thomas Weld who became a cardinal, and Joseph Weld who spent £30,000 at Inman's yard on the Lymington river on his three famous yachts *The Arrow, The Lulworth* and *The Alarm*. Pylewell Park was the scene of a balloon ascent in 1785 manned by Vincenzo Lunardi, known as 'The apostle of aerostation'. The artist Thomas Rowlandson was visiting the house at the time. The mansion has always played an important part in the life of the area.

**The New Forest:** In 1079 William the Conqueror declared that all the land from the Wiltshire Downs south to the Solent, from Southampton Water and west to the Avon valley, should be his own hunting forest, preserved for the deer to roam freely and never farmed. Harsh forest laws were applied to trespassers and the Saxon Chroniclers derisively termed the land, formerly called Ytene, the New Forest. Today, over 100 square miles of this medieval landscape of rolling heaths and woods – some very old, mainly of oaks and beeches known as Ancient and Ornamental – survive for all to enjoy.

There is a great deal to delight the rambler in the New Forest. Gradually the Forest Commoners regained their ancient rights to pasture their animals and care for the semi-wild ponies that preserve the open heath and soft green Forest lawns. Other rights include the right to spread marl and gather fuel.

Apart from the ponies and their charming leggy foals, the Forest is home for many other animals including red, fallow, roe and sika deer and a large population of badgers. Woodland birds include some rarities such as the lesser spotted woodpecker and birds of the open heath include Dartford warblers. The wild gladiolus grows among the bracken under the oak trees whose upper branches are still frequented by the very rare purple emperor butterfly.

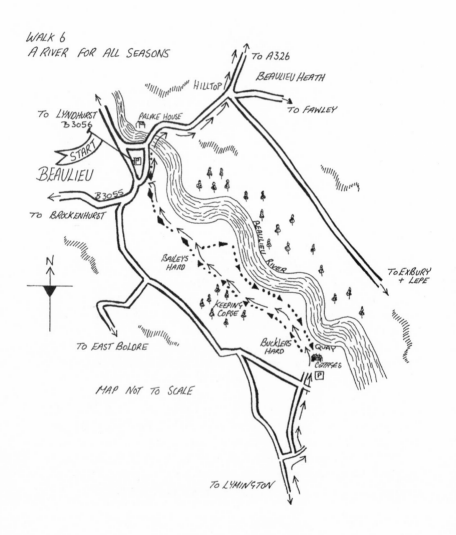

WALK 6
A RIVER FOR ALL SEASONS

To A326
BEAULIEU HEATH

HILLTOP

To FAWLEY

PALACE HOUSE

To LYNDHURST
B3056

START

BEAULIEU

B3055

To BROCKENHURST

BEAULIEU RIVER

BAILEYS
HARD

N

To EXBURY
+ LEPE

KEEPING
COPSE

To EAST BOLDRE

BUCKLERS
HARD

QUAY

COTTAGES

P

MAP NOT TO SCALE

To LYMINGTON

# A river for all seasons –
# the Beaulieu river
## (Solent Way – Sowley Brooms crosstrack to Beaulieu village)

**Introduction:** This short walk connects two of the most fascinating places in the New Forest, Beaulieu and Bucklers Hard. 'Beaulieu' means 'beautiful place' and this ramble beside the Beaulieu river passes through the woods and fields which made the perfect backdrop for the film of Robert Bolt's play *A Man for all Seasons*. The river was the nearest approach that could be found today to the leafy banks of the Thames near Chelsea as it was in the 16th century. Even now, as yachts and dinghies throng the river, shelduck families glide among the inlets, curlews, redshanks and oystercatchers wade along the edges of the saltmarsh and terns perform their flying displays overhead. On quiet summer evenings nightingales still sing in the Beaulieu woods.

The walk begins in Beaulieu village close to the ruins of the great Cistercian Abbey founded here in 1204. The Abbey property, including a unique right to the bed of the Beaulieu river, passed into lay hands at the Dissolution and is now owned by Lord Montagu. The gatehouse of the Abbey has been converted into his home, Palace House, and is open to the public. The estate also houses the National Motor Museum.

The visit to Bucklers Hard reveals another aspect of the river. The village is tiny, just a double row of 18th century cottages built of rich red bricks, facing each other across wide greens sloping down to the water. Today it is a peaceful scene, an ideal spot for picnics and what Ratty in *The Wind in the Willows* called 'just messing about in boats'. But once it bustled with life and was noisy with the rasp of saws, the thud of hammers and the shouts of workmen as they shaped the great hulls of the warships for Nelson's fleet. The old

53

slipways remain and a museum in one of the village's former inns recreates that world with interiors of inn scenes and cottages of the 1790s.

There is so much to see on this walk and at Bucklers Hard that I would recommend visiting Palace House, the Abbey ruins and the National Motor Museum at Beaulieu on a separate occasion. This is a walk for all seasons but the river is at its best in early spring and autumn.

**Distance:** Sowley Brooms crosstrack to Beaulieu on the Solent Way 7 miles. Circular walk 4.5 miles. OS Landranger series 1:50 000 map 196 The Solent. Also OS map 22 New Forest in the Outdoor Leisure series. Part of the circular walk beside the Beaulieu river is not marked on the OS map but it is a clearly marked public footpath.

**Refreshments:** In Beaulieu village the Montagu Arms and the Old Bakehouse tearooms, which also serves lunches. In the Beaulieu visitor centre, which includes Palace House, the National Motor Museum and Abbey ruins, there is a café and licensed restaurant.

The centre is open every day, except Christmas Day, at 10 am, and closes between 5 pm and 7 pm, depending on the season.

At Bucklers Hard the Master Builder's hotel has a public bar which welcomes walkers and within the Maritime Museum complex there is a café and licensed restaurant.

The Museum is open every day from 10 am to 6 pm Easter to Spring Bank Holiday, from 10 am to 9 pm Spring Bank Holiday to September, and from 10 am to 4.30 pm winter months to Easter (closed Christmas Day). The cottages close at 6 pm. The cafeteria is open daily, 10 am to 6 pm, Easter to October.

**Beaulieu river cruises:** River cruises lasting half an hour in the motorboat *Swiftsure* depart from the pier at Bucklers Hard from Easter to October. Departure times are advertised at the pier kiosk.

**How to get there:** From Lyndhurst, follow the Beaulieu road, the B3056. The road passes the entrance to Beaulieu visitor centre and National Motor Museum. Shortly after, turn left following the sign for Beaulieu village. The car park is on your right before you reach the main street. If this car park is full start the circular walk from Bucklers Hard instead. Turn right and drive up Beaulieu High Street following the one-way system. Turn left to rejoin the B3056 and drive in the direction of Lymington. Almost immediately the road turns right. Leave the B3056, bearing a little left for Bucklers Hard where you will find large car parks.

Wilts and Dorset run a bus service to Beaulieu from Hythe and Lymington. Ring 0202 673555 for details.

**Solent Way – Sowley Brooms crosstrack to Beaulieu village:** When the route of Walk Five turns left at the crosstrack on the edge of Sowley Brooms wood keep straight on with a field on your right. Over the fields, as you follow the Way to Bucklers Hard, there are occasional views of the Solent shimmering in the distance against a background of the Isle of Wight hills. Turn right as directed at the next hedge and walk towards the lane with the hedge on your right, then turn left, parallel with the lane, along the edge of a field. This leads to a small wooden gate on the right which opens into the lane. Go through the gate, turn left and continue along the lane towards Sowley Pond.

The Cistercian monks who built Beaulieu Abbey required a great deal of fish and dammed several small streams to create the pond. Today woods fringe its shores and it is a haven for wildlife, but in the 17th and 18th centuries there was an ironworks here. The water powered tilt-hammers which worked the ironstone from Hengistbury Head and the beaches at Hordle.

Follow the lane to a T-junction and turn right for Bucklers Hard. The Cistercians would have used much of their land – now the Beaulieu Manor estate – for grazing their sheep, and the house called Bergerie, French for a sheep-farm, recalls those days. Another reminder is the ruins at St Leonards which you pass a little later. This was a grange for the lay brothers who worked the fields. Close to the road is the east end of a huge barn once used to store the produce with a modern barn built within its confines. Over the wall, across the field close to Grange House, are the ruins of the lay brothers' chapel, still preserving a little delicate tracery within a window arch.

Shortly after St Leonards, the Way turns right then bears left to follow a very narrow lane to Bucklers Hard. Walk carefully here as there is very little room for a pedestrian. Fortunately this dangerous lane leads in about a ¼ mile to Bucklers Hard village. Cross the stile and walk down to the river. Follow the route of Walk Six to Beaulieu. (Either reverse the route as described from Beaulieu to Bucklers Hard along the river bank, or take the quicker return track.) Then turn to Walk Seven.

**The Walk:** From the car park in Beaulieu village, a narrow gravelled path runs to the right, past the Old Bakehouse tea rooms to the village street. Beaulieu is an enchanting village of mainly 18th century houses. Bear left down the street and now you have a lovely view over the river and the mill pond to the low stone walls encircling the precincts of the Abbey with the porter's lodge over the gate. Green lawns, golden with daffodils in spring, slope down to the water's edge. There is a glimpse of the towers of Palace House among the trees and the little church which was originally the monks' refectory.

Cross the street in front of the Montagu Arms and follow the footpath sign to the left of the hotel. The former mill, which only ceased grinding the villagers' corn in 1927, is on your left. The track leads round the hotel to a stile and continues over fields with the river a silver ribbon winding through woodlands into the distance. Here the river scenes for *A Man for all Seasons* were filmed. The film crew built a replica of the garden wall of Sir Thomas More's house on the river bank and local people joined the cast as extras.

The gravelled track becomes a wide grassy way and slopes down to an inlet. A narrow gravelled path leads round the rushes beside the water then rises to follow the side of fields with a tall hedge on the left. These fields were first farmed by the monks of Beaulieu Abbey.

Soon you will see Brickyard Cottage ahead and the chimneys of the old brickworks, established in 1790, close to the river. Past the cottage the path skirts another inlet, Baileys Hard. It was here, in 1696, that Richard Herring obtained a contract to build the *Salisbury* of 48 guns, the first warship to be built on the Beaulieu river. During the last war, which brought great activity to the river, a wooden minesweeper was built here. Just after a private gravel track joins on the left, the walk bears right. Turn left for Bucklers Hard following the footpath sign.

Now a straight track runs through the woods to the village, but there is a little path that winds through the trees along the river bank which is the route of the walk. You must look carefully to find it. After the left turn, continue along the straight track for about 200 yards until the track crosses a small stream. Over the stream, turn immediately left through the woods along a small path – difficult to see under fallen leaves – with the stream at first on your left. This leads through oaks and beeches to the river bank. Now the walk is really beautiful as you tread in the footsteps of the monks, and in later centuries those of generations of shipyard workers. Beyond the shore at low tide stretch banks of reed-fringed saltmarsh spiked with Townsend's grass, a form of cordgrass which appeared in this area in 1870. Many other saltmarsh flowers colour the marsh, especially sea lavender. The path curves right to leave the bank of the river and join the gravel track again at the entrance to the woods of Keeping Copse. Follow the track as it leads a little right then over the marshes towards Bucklers Hard. You pass the yacht marina and come to a small road. Cross, and look for a narrow footpath a little to your left on the other side. Follow this as it leads down to the riverside once more.

As you approach the village you pass an intriguing thatched building with a small pool. The third Duke of Montagu built this in 1760 to enable his son to enjoy salt water bathing throughout the year.

You pass the old slipways where warships were once built as you turn to walk up the little street running between two rows of small 18th century cottages which is Bucklers Hard village. As the result of careful management, very little seems to have changed here in the last 190 years. Overlooking the water on your right is the Master Builder's house and if you look in the window of his study you will see the figure of the master builder himself, Henry Adams, a glass of wine at his elbow, discussing the plans of his latest warship with one of the Navy Board overseers. A little further up the street is a little chapel dedicated to St Mary, patron of all seafarers. It was once the cobbler's shop and later the village school.

Call in next door at No 80 to enjoy a reconstruction of scenes in a shipwright's cottage. And before leaving, a visit to the museum at the top of the street is a must. It tells the whole story of Bucklers Hard with models of the village and the ships which were built there. You step back to the end of the 18th century as you enter the bar of the New Inn busy with well-known figures from that time and share the problems of a poor labourer in his primitive cottage. To return to Beaulieu along the Solent Way retrace your steps to the waterside and follow the former route to the entrance to Keeping Copse where the track divides. You can of course take the little path by the riverside that you followed earlier, but for a quicker route and a change of scene continue straight on along the woodland track – the Solent Way. Just before the stream the riverside path meets the track on the right. Continue along your former route, following the Solent Way sign, back to Beaulieu.

## Historical Notes

**Beaulieu Manor Estate:** Ever since 1079, when William the Conqueror declared the land between Southampton Water and the Avon Valley to be his own special hunting reserve, his New Forest, most of this area has remained the property of the monarch. So it is surprising to find this huge Estate of over 10,000 acres in private hands. The ancestors of Lord Montagu who owns the land today bought the estate when the monasteries were dissolved in 1538. But how did the monastery, with all its lands including such a prize as the river, come to be there in the first place?

According to the Saxon Chroniclers, in 1204 twelve Cistercian monks approached King John with a request for land on which to build a monastery. He refused and ordered his horsemen to trample the monks to death. They would not obey him and the King retired for the night, furious. That night he dreamed he was hauled before the judgement seat of God and suffered dreadfully for his sins. In the morning, a contrite King granted the monks the large estates beside the Beaulieu river we see today and a unique right to the bed of the river which meant they could charge tariffs on all waterborne trade. Extraordinary though this story is, it is an undeniable fact that King John was notably irreligious and only endowed one other monastic establishment.

The monks built a huge church, the size of York Minster, the outline of which you can still trace today. They grew rich trading their wool and were completely self-supporting. They cared for the sick, educated the children, sheltered travellers and offered the right of sanctuary to all fugitives. Although much of the stone was carted away to build coastal defences the ruined cloisters are still lovely and some buildings remain. The first floor of the building where the monks slept, now called the Domus, is used for banquets, and the ground floor, originally a dining hall for the lay brothers, contains an exhibition of monastic life. The monks' refectory is now the parish church.

Palace House is welcoming and most unusual. It was carefully planned in the 1870s to incorporate the large Abbey gatehouse with its central arches through which visitors to the Abbey originally passed. Splendid drawing rooms and dining halls can be viewed and some fine pictures which include a small portrait of Charles II.

**The Beaulieu river:** The river rises in the heart of the New Forest, near Lyndhurst. Through the centuries it has seen a great variety of ships: trading vessels in medieval times which docked at the wharf in Beaulieu in front of the Abbey, the hulls of warships being towed to Portsmouth for fitting out, and nowadays a multitude of pleasure craft. It is the home of the Beaulieu River Sailing Club and the Royal Southampton Yacht Club.

The river played its part in both world wars. During the First World War, Fairmile motor launches were built at Bucklers Hard, and during the Second World War the village became once more a busy shipbuilding centre, assembling motor torpedo boats from prefabricated sections brought by rail from Beaulieu Road station. Downstream, deep basins originally cut into the river bank for breeding oysters were used to construct parts for the Mulberry harbours vital for the Allied landings in Normandy on D-Day. The Royal Marines, famous as 'The Cockleshell Heroes', practised on the river. Neville Shute's novel *Requiem for a Wren* vividly portrays those wartime days around Beaulieu.

**Bucklers Hard:** The survival of this historic village in its present form is due to careful planning today and the action of the French navy in the past.

John, second Duke of Montagu, intended Bucklers Hard to be Montagu town, a sugar-refining community, the raw material being brought over from newly created plantations in the West Indies. He sent an expedition of seven ships to St Lucia but unfortunately the French navy drove his colonists off the island with a superior force.

The construction of Montagu town had begun; forest had been

cleared and a few cottages built either side of a street leading down to the river. The Duke knew the site was ideal. Whatever the state of the tide the river was deep enough to take ships drawing up to five feet, and at this point on the river bank there were gravel beds strong enough to provide support for slipways. Although Montagu town was never realised, the shipbuilders came and in 1745 the warship HMS *Surprise* was launched at Bucklers Hard. Many more were to follow including Nelson's favourite ship HMS *Agamemnon*, or 'Am and Eggs' as her crew called her.

# By the Dark Water – one of the New Forest's hidden valleys

## (Solent Way – Beaulieu village to Hill Top)

**Introduction:** The Dark Water valley is hidden in the south-east corner of the New Forest, away from the usual tourist routes. Although Fawley Power Station is barely two miles away over the heath, this walk reveals the Forest at its magical best, a medieval landscape of heathland and commons, tree-shaded streams and ancient oak woods.

Four thousand years ago the people of the Bronze Age lived in the Dark Water valley and buried their dead in the many tumuli or barrows that dot the heath on either side. To reach the valley, the walk follows the route of a road along which the Britons traded Cornish tin, Welsh gold and lead from the Mendip hills long before the Romans built their trading port at Lepe where the Dark Water flows into the Solent.

The naturalist W.H. Hudson (see Historical Notes on p. 65) described many happy hours observing wildlife in the valley. For him, the valley and surrounding heaths and woods were 'a favourite summer resort'. Even today, with modern industry so close, the valley is a special place.

**Distance:** Beaulieu village to Hill Top on the Solent Way 1 mile. Circular walk 7.5 miles. OS Landranger series 1:50 000 map 196 The Solent. OS Outdoor Leisure series 1:25 000 map 22 New Forest.

**Refreshments:** Cafés and inn, the Montagu Arms, in Beaulieu village. The Bridge Tavern beside the Fawley road (circular walk only).

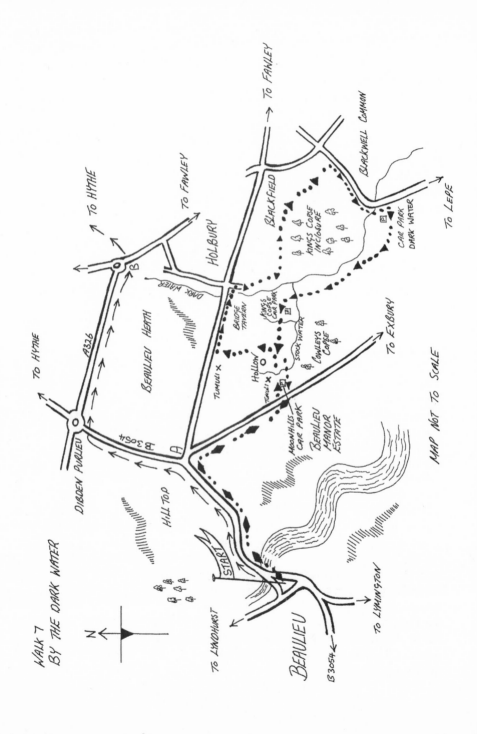

WALK 7
BY THE DARK WATER

N

MAP NOT TO SCALE

TO HYTHE

TO HYTHE

DIBDEN PURLIEU

A326

B3054

HILL TOP

START

TO LYNDHURST

BEAULIEU

B3054

TO LYMINGTON

TO EXBURY

BEAULIEU MANOR ESTATE

MOONHILLS CAR PARK

TUMULI ×

TUMULI ×

HOLLOW

STOCK WATER

COWLEY'S COPSE

BEAULIEU HEATH

DARK WATER

TO FAWLEY

HOLBURY

BRIDGE TAVERN

KING'S COPSE CAR PARK

KING'S COPSE INCLOSURE

BLACKFIELD

TO FAWLEY

BLACKWELL COMMON

DARK WATER

CAR PARK

TO LEPE

**How to get there:** The walk starts from the car park in Beaulieu village. Approaching from Lyndhurst along the B3056, turn left for Beaulieu village just past the entrance to the Motor Museum. The car park is signed on the right.

**Solent Way – Beaulieu village to Hill Top:** Walk down Beaulieu village High Street towards the river and cross with the mill on your right. Bear right along the road, past Palace House and the Abbey gatehouse, following the route of Walk Seven as far as Hill Top. Now turn to Walk Eight.

**The Walk:** Leave the car park in Beaulieu village by the main entrance and turn right to the foot of the High Street, opposite the Montagu Arms. Bear left to cross the river. Palace House, the home of Lord Montagu, stands above lawns sloping down to the monks' former fish pond on the left. Follow the road, B3054, as it curves right past the walls of the ruined Abbey precinct. Opposite, wide greens fringe the mill pond.

The road climbs gently to a junction with a minor road for Fawley at Hill Top. Here the walk leaves the Solent Way. Turn right along the minor road for just a few yards where it is joined by another minor road, for Exbury, on the right. Bear right along the Exbury Road until you come to Moonhills car park on the left. Turn left and walk straight on over the parking area to its most northerly point. Now follow the clear path that runs over the heath on your right towards a group of low Bronze Age burial mounds.

Past the mounds, the path bears half-right over the heath to the birch and oak woods fringing Cowleys Copse, then it bears a little left through the trees before dipping to cross a bridge over a stream, Stock Water. Now for some careful navigation! Climb the slope ahead and look for a large, circular hollow on your left (it is about a hundred yards from the bridge). Turn left to follow a faint path round the right-hand edge of the hollow and walk under some power lines. Now take the good path ahead leading north over Beaulieu Heath. Go straight over a crosstrack and continue to meet the Fawley road just to the right of another cluster of Bronze Age burial mounds. Turn right and walk beside the road on the open heath. The road dips to cross a bridge over the Dark Water beside the Bridge Tavern. Walk up the hill ahead – there is a narrow verge but children may need watching for these few yards – and at the top the walk leaves the road to turn right along the track opposite Park Lane. But before turning right it is rewarding to cross the road to look down into the meadows beside the Dark Water. The ridges and embankments marking the site of Holbury Manor, which in medieval times was held by the monks of Beaulieu Abbey, are still clearly visible. 'Holbury' means a fortress in a hollow and the village close by was once a flourishing Roman settlement.

Follow the footpath sign down the track to the right of the road. This leafy pathway, overlooking fields, running along the eastern boundary of the New Forest, divides two contrasting worlds. The track turns left opposite the gates of Greenrollestone Estate to run beside a wood, thickly carpeted with bluebells. Go through a gate and past a joining track on the left to continue along a very wide, raised greenway, firm underfoot, part I am sure, of the route of an ancient British road.

Follow the greenway round a right turn and straight on to cross over a lane. Continue over the heath, Blackwell Common, to the Exbury road. Turn right and walk towards the dark line of the woods of Kings Copse Inclosure which clothe the Dark Water valley. The road runs down to a bridge over the Dark Water where the trees crowd close to the bank. Cross the bridge and walk up the hill ahead through the trees. After about 50 yards turn right into the Dark Water car park. Cross the parking area and keep straight on along a woodland path. There is a fence on the embankment on your left and after a few yards it is wise to follow the little path up the bank and continue close to the fence as the main path can be muddy at this point. The path bears right to join the main track and go through a gate into Kings Copse Inclosure, a beautiful old wood with a variety of trees tangled with honeysuckle, ivies and wild roses. In spring, the ground is purple with violets.

Just beyond the gate the path divides. Follow the right-hand path along the side of the Dark Water valley. The stream is invisible as yet beneath a screen of willows and oaks. Keep to the main path, ignoring all joining paths on the left. Like most Forest ways, the main path has a tendency to twist about awkwardly so if in doubt, bear right!

When you come to a crosstrack – you will see the track on the right leading down to a bridge over the Dark Water – keep straight on along a secluded green path. This leads down to a bridge over the stream. Cross, and climb through the trees to a gate leading out of the Inclosure. Walk over Kings Copse car park but do not follow the gravel track continuing ahead. Instead, turn left and walk through the trees with the fence enclosing the woods of Kings Copse on your left and Beaulieu Heath on your right. The path leads over a footbridge and meets the path followed early in the walk past Cowleys Copse. Retrace your steps over the stream, bearing half right to Moonhills car park before following the Exbury road back to Hill Top and turning left for Beaulieu village.

## Historical Notes

**Ancient British Road:** Unlike most woodland tracks this wide greenway runs in a straight and determined fashion towards the old trading port near Lepe or Stone Point. I believe it is a continuation of the known British track that can be seen running through Fawley Inclosure north of the very ancient settlement of Holbury to the east of Beaulieu Heath. It is directly in line with that road. This area of the New Forest has been inhabited since earliest times. Mesolithic and Neolithic peoples hunted in the Dark Water valley. Three hundred of their flint tools have been found.

**W.H. Hudson:** A fascinating character and a very fine naturalist, William Henry Hudson was born in Argentina – his parents were American of English descent – in 1841. He arrived in England in 1869 and fell in love with the English countryside. He visited the New Forest and rented Roydon Manor near Boldre which he describes in his book *Hampshire Days*. He spent most of his time observing wildlife on Beaulieu Heath and in the Dark Water valley. Sitting by the stream he writes: 'I sought and found the stream well named the Dark Water; here it is grown over with old ivied oaks, with brambles and briars that throw long branches from side to side, making the almost hidden current in the deep shade look black; but when the sunlight falls on it the water is the colour of old sherry from the red soil it flows over.'

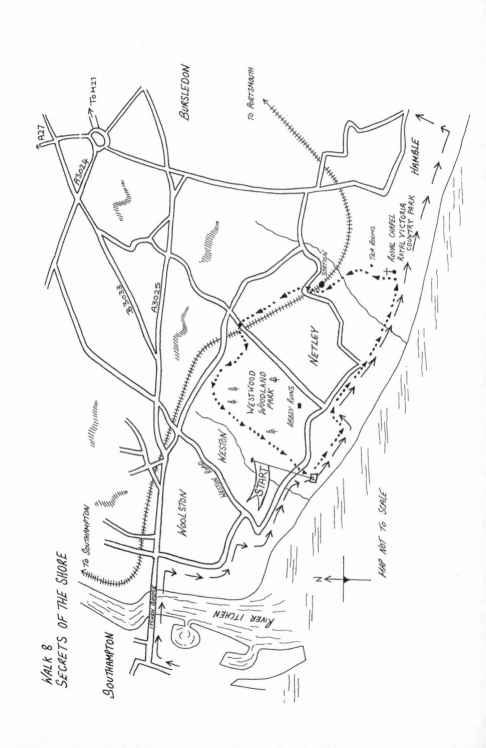

WALK 8
SECRETS OF THE SHORE

SOUTHAMPTON

BURSLEDON

TO PORTSMOUTH

HAMBLE

A27

TO M27

A3024

B3033

A3025

TO SOUTHAMPTON

ITCHEN BRIDGE

WOOLSTON

WESTON

WESTON

START

RIVER ITCHEN

WESTWOOD WOODLAND PARK

ABBEY RUINS

NETLEY

STATION

TEA ROOMS

ROYAL CHAPEL

ROYAL VICTORIA COUNTRY PARK

MAP NOT TO SCALE

N

# Secrets of the shore – Netley Abbey, Royal Victoria Country Park and Westwood Woodland Park

(Solent Way – Hill Top through Southampton to the Royal Victoria Country Park)

**Introduction:** Although this circular walk close to Southampton Water is very short – less than 4 miles – there is so much to see and enjoy that I suggest packing a picnic and taking a full day. It is an ideal family walk as there is something to please everyone. History comes alive in the romantic ruins of Netley Abbey and in the Royal Victoria Country Park, which was once the site of a great military hospital. Now it is a large landscaped area, open to all, with a museum re-creating life in Victorian times.

Children will enjoy combing the beach for shells – the Park beach is a specially good place for this – and rides on a miniature steam railway. The chapel for the former hospital has been preserved and from the top of the tower there is a breathtaking view of Southampton Water and its shipping from the western docks to Calshot Spit.

Leaving the New Forest, the Solent Way continues by ferry from Hythe to Southampton, crosses the Itchen Bridge and reaches the eastern shore of Southampton Water at Woolston. The walk begins about a mile further on, joining the Solent Way to follow the shoreline as far as the Royal Victoria Country Park. From the Park, the walk turns inland to explore Westwood Woodland Park. Signposted paths lead through old woods, imaginatively merged with recently established grassland. If you are a nature lover this could well be the highlight of your walk.

**Distance:** Hill Top through Southampton to the Royal Victoria Country Park on the Solent Way 9 miles. Circular walk just under 4 miles. OS Landranger Series 1:50 000 map 196 The Solent. OS Outdoor Leisure series 1:25 000 map 22 New Forest.

**Refreshments:** Netley offers all facilities, including the Prince Consort pub which does hot meals, while the Royal Victoria Country Park has tearooms and a sheltered picnic area. The walk passes the Station pub at Netley and just before the entrance to Westwood Woodland Park is the Grange Inn. There is a picnic area in Westwood.

**How to get there:** The walk starts from the car park on Weston Shore, close to Westwood and the ruins of Netley Abbey. From Southampton, head east along the A3025 over the Itchen bridge (toll). Continue straight on for about a mile until the A3025 turns left under a railway bridge. Leave the A3025 and keep straight on following the sign for Weston Shore. At the next roundabout (under ¼ mile) turn right down Weston Lane and drive straight on down to the shore. Ignore the car park ahead, and follow the road left for about ½ mile. Park in the car park on your right facing Southampton Water, just before you come to the trees of Westwood.

The start is easily reached from the M27. Leave at junction 8 and follow the signs for the Royal Victoria Country Park. Continue down Weston Lane and park as directed above.

Netley is served by Wilts and Dorset buses and you could start this circular walk from Netley station which is on the main Southampton-Portsmouth line.

**Solent Way – Hill Top through Southampton to the Royal Victoria Country Park:** At present the Solent Way continues from Hill Top (marked A on the map for Walk 7) along the B3054 over Beaulieu Heath to meet the main Fawley road (A326) close to the roundabout at Dibden Purlieu. Before the roundabout, by the cattle grid, bear right, south-east, to follow the Forest edge, with the road on the left for about 1½ miles to the next roundabout at Hardley (marked B on the map for Walk 7). This part of the Solent Way may be re-routed so look for new waymarking signs at Hill Top.

Just past the Hardley roundabout cross the main road (A326) and keep straight on down the lane ahead with the Forest Home pub on your right. After about 100 yards go straight over the crossroads towards the Esso depot (Hythe Terminal). Continue for a few yards before turning left along a footpath. The path curves right then left and becomes a country lane with views over some of the small woods and valleys that have survived the industrial development along this shore.

Keep straight on past a joining track on the left and when the main track turns right a little further on follow the lane straight ahead. The lane fringes woodland before dipping to cross a small bridge and climbing past the Travellers Rest pub. Continue along the made road – Hart Hill – and turn right when you meet a crossing road. Now Southampton Water is ahead and from the shore there are splendid views north to Southampton's eastern docks and south to the oil terminal at Hamble.

The road bears left to follow the shoreline past extensive saltmarshes, a nature reserve, towards some large grey sheds. In the days of the flying boats these huge sheds were used for maintenance. Keep straight on into the village and turn right following the signs to the ferry on the waterfront. This leaves from the pier, which runs for 2,000 feet into Southampton Water and dates from 1880. Thankfully, there is a narrow gauge railway to save your feet. The ferry from Hythe berths at Southampton's Town Quay. From the terminal turn right and walk through the complex of shops and restaurants to the waterfront. The Solent Way is not marked through Southampton, so I would suggest the following for a quick and interesting route.

Cross the main road immediately opposite the entrance to Town Quay to see part of Southampton's medieval walls adjoining the 15th century Watergate in Porter's Lane. Here merchants trading English wool for wines from the Mediterranean and spices and silks from the east paid their taxes. On the right are the ruins of a Norman merchant's house and if you wish you could start a tour of Southampton's old city walls from this point.

To continue the Way, cross the High Street and turn down Winkle Street, an appropriate name for this narrow medieval alley. Walk through God's House Gate, built in the 13th century and named after a 12th century hospice for pilgrims. Adjoining is

God's House Tower, built in the 15th century to protect the sluice gates which controlled the flow of water into the town moat. Now the buildings house Southampton's Museum of Archaeology.

Continue along Platform Road and Canute Road – reputedly where Canute demonstrated he could not turn back the tide – past South Western House. In the days of the great liners this was the railway terminus hotel and the lines remain which ran into the hotel, across the road, straight to the docks. Turn left into Royal Crescent, then right into Albert Road South. On your left stands Southampton's Hall of Aviation incorporating the Mitchell Museum.

Climb the steps at the end of the road to cross the Itchen Bridge and descend the steps at the other side into Woolston. Bear right along Bridge Road, cross Portsmouth Road and continue down Victoria Road past the Vosper Thorneycroft naval shipbuilding yards to Southampton Water at Weston Point. Bear left past the sailing club and now a pleasant waterside path leads to the car park at the start of Walk Eight. Follow the route of this walk as far as the Royal Victoria Park then turn to Walk Nine.

**The Walk:** With Southampton Water on your right, leave the car park and take the little path running beneath oak trees close to the shore. Wading birds follow the ebbing tide, picking at the mud between the gravel which overlays the eastern shore of Southampton Water as far as Hamble Common. Continue along the sea front and beach past Netley Castle, now a convalescent home. The original castle, built by Henry VIII in 1542 as part of his coastal defences, has vanished within a large Victorian mansion built in the 1880s, although it is possible that the Tudor archway in the main entrance was part of the fort. Bear left over the recreation ground to the road.

Over the road to your left is the entrance to the ruins of Netley Abbey. Set in a shallow valley overlooking the waterside and shaded by huge oaks and beeches, the ruined Abbey is a beautiful sight even from the road. But it is worth exploring further as a great deal of the graceful 13th century work remains, particularly the soaring arches and windows of the Abbey church. At the request of the Bishop of Winchester, Cistercian monks from Beaulieu landed here in 1239 to establish the Abbey and later King Henry III became their patron.

From the Abbey, walk on up the hill towards Netley village. When you come to Grange Road you might like to leave the Solent Way for a moment and turn left to look at Netley church. It is a fine example of Victorian architecture, with a splendid timbered roof. Return to the shore road to continue to Netley. On the right of the road, in front of a wide grassed area, is a horse trough complete with its own small wooden pump. Netley village is described by Pevsner as 'a Victorian period piece' and so it is. Impressive family villas overlook the shore and facing them across the road are rows of terraced cottages, many of them attractively renovated.

When the main road bears left, keep straight on following the signs for the Royal Victoria Country Park. You pass a splendidly Victorian pub, the Prince Consort. Several small streams flow down to the Solent over its eastern shore and just before you come to the Park entrance you will see that one of them has been channelled into a series of small lakes providing a haven for ducks and geese. In front of the Park gates is part of Netley Hard, which dates from the 13th century. In the past it was the scene of great activity, including the famous Netley Regatta. Follow the road into the Royal Victoria Country Park and when the road divides keep straight on over the grass under the pines towards the chapel of the former Royal Victoria Military Hospital.

Wide grassland and terraces spread to a distant line of woods and sweep down to the shore fringed by pines. Everywhere there are beautiful trees and shrubs, favourites of the Victorian gardeners who laid out the grounds of the former hospital. The hospital was demolished in 1966 after 110 years of service, and since the purchase of the whole site in 1980 by the County Council these grounds of over 200 acres have been open to all.

The Royal Chapel with its conspicuous green dome, once the centrepiece of the hospital, has been preserved and is now a museum housing displays detailing the history of the hospital since the Crimean War. The hospital was one of Queen Victoria's favourite projects. She laid the foundation stone and the display shows her visiting the wards.

From a platform in the chapel dome you have a magnificent view of Southampton Water, one of the great historic waterways of the world. There is always a wealth of shipping to be seen, including container ships from Southampton's newer western docks, huge oil tankers from the Gulf moored off the oil refinery's terminal at Fawley, ferries to the old Forest port of Hythe, the Isle of Wight and the Continent, dredgers, tugs, pilot vessels, fishing boats and a colourful array of yachts and motorboats. The days of the great liners that sometimes had to wait their turn to dock at Southampton's Ocean Terminal may have gone, but the port is still popular with visiting cruise ships. You may see the *Canberra* or the *Queen Elizabeth 2* sailing to or from her own terminal opened by the Queen in 1966. The opposite shore appears heavily industrialised from Calshot in the south, where Henry VIII's small castle is dwarfed by the chimneys of a great oil-fired power station, past Fawley Refinery with its associated petro-chemical works and on to Marchwood Military Port, but you can still see glimpses of the Forest trees that once fringed the waterside.

A path runs along the Park shoreline for almost a mile. The old pierhead where the wounded from the Crimea were ferried ashore remains clearly visible. Another building to survive is the officers' mess.

The Park is a specially good place for children. There are shells to be collected on the beach, woodland walks, a playground and, best of all, a narrow-gauge railway using both diesel and steam engines, which provides a delightful trip through some of the Park's most scenic areas. Take this trip at bluebell time!

Our walk leaves the Solent Way, which follows the shoreline, and continues from the Park's tearooms, which are housed in the large wooden building you will see to the north of the chapel. This was formerly the old hospital YMCA donated by the British Timber Association. Inside the Empire Room is a dado of rare woods. The walk leaves the park by the Hound Gate north of the tearooms. With your back to the shore and the tearooms on your right take the footpath leading ahead between pine trees. There is a car park on your left. This leads to an asphalt road. Continue straight on past Hound Lodge downhill. About 100 yards past the lodge you will see a narrow footpath on the left with a prominent 'no cycling' sign which is our way. But before turning left look closely at the road on the right to see pieces of the old track of the branch line which brought many of the wounded to the former hospital.

The footpath runs along the top of a wooded valley to Netley station. Bear left then right round the Station pub to St Mary's Road. Walk up to the bridge over the line and cross to a footpath on the left. Take this path between the line on your left and houses on your right until it bears right to bring you to Grange Road. Turn left beside the road to cross the bridge and walk towards the red-brick Grange pub. (This is only about 100 yards and there is a grass verge apart from the bridge where you need to watch for traffic.)

Just before the Grange a wooden gate on your right leads you into Westwood Woodland Park. Follow the track for Weston Shore as it winds left over Grange Fields to lead you into what I am sure is one of the Solent's most fascinating areas, 'Southampton's Secret Woodland'. To walk through Westwood is to step back in time 800 years and enjoy a landscape that has changed little since the Cistercian monks lived and worked there. The Westwood Rangers have cared for Westwood since 1987 and introduced some surprises.

Leave the grass to follow the little woodland path into Bluebell Wood. The path dips over one of the deep ditches – originally watercourses or conduits – dug by the monks to channel water to their fishponds. When the path divides follow the path ahead deeper into this ancient oak wood with sunny glades full of flowers. Less common plants include the drooping sprays of Solomon's seal and you will see some interesting trees. Among them are wild service trees covered with white flowers in May followed by brownish-red fruits like tiny apples beloved by birds, and sessile oaks which can be distinguished by their stalkless acorns. These flourish in Bluebell Wood because until 1970 it was pasture woodland grazed by farm animals.

When the path divides again turn right (there are two possible paths which meet later) following the sign for Weston Shore. Keep to the path through the woods, past a sign directing you to the oldest tree, to a more open area. Follow the gravelled path as it turns left and leads to steps past a picnic site on the right. Tables have been provided and this is a good place at which to pause and climb up the mound to the viewpoint. From here, on a clear day, it is possible to see the clock on Southampton Civic Centre, Bitterne church, Fawley power station, Hythe marina, the tower of the Royal Chapel in the Royal Victoria Country Park and the crane at

Vosper Thorneycroft's shipyard at Woolston.

Return to our original path to the left of the picnic site and keep straight on to another choice of ways. Weston Shore is directly ahead, but to see one of the Park's surprises turn left for the water garden. Soon the path bears right downhill to reveal a watery world of lakes and islands. This Victorian water garden was restored by the Rangers in 1989. Tall stands of reeds and attractively variegated bamboo are home to ducks and moorhens and you may catch a glimpse of the Westwood kingfisher.

Bear right and cross the bridge to climb the steps to a wide path which runs through coppiced woodland. Turn left and follow the path to the road beside Weston Shore. Cross the road and turn right to retrace your steps through the trees back to your car.

## Historical Notes

**Netley Abbey:** The whole of this walk crosses lands that once belonged to the Abbey. Very little is known of its earlier history as the records were destroyed but the survival of so much of the church is explained by the Tudor brickwork which is built into its grey stones. In 1536, after the Dissolution, the estate was granted to Sir William Paulet who converted the Abbey into a mansion. The south transept became his great hall with a screened-off kitchen, and it is said that he used the nave as a tennis court and stabled his horses in the monks' refectory. The mansion was inhabited until 1700 but today only traces of brickwork remain.

In the 18th century the whole estate was owned by Thomas Chamberlayne, a kindly man who won the approval of William Cobbett. He recorded the pleasure he gained from roaming in the fields and woods in his famous book *Rural Rides*.

Now the Abbey is cared for by English Heritage and is open from Easter to the end of September, 10 am to 1 pm and 2 pm to 6 pm. During the rest of the year it is open weekends only, the gate closing at 4 pm.

**Royal Victoria Country Park:** Reaction to the horrors of the Crimean War led to the building of the Royal Victoria Military Hospital. It was a huge building designed more to impress the onlooker than to provide a convenient place in which to work. As

Florence Nightingale pointed out, the corridors – over a ¼ mile in length – faced west with views over the water, while the wards faced inwards towards the orderlies' quarters.

The hospital saw service throughout the Boer War and the two world wars. It was one of the main centres of the Royal Army Medical Corps and the laboratories contributed much to medical research, especially in the field of tropical diseases. In the First World War, Netley became No 1 base hospital and a huge Red Cross complex was built in the grounds. In 1942 the hospital was taken over by the Americans, who are said to have driven jeeps up the long corridors.

The hospital may have gone but the grounds remain. Corsican, Scots and Monterey pines shelter the roads and fringe the shore. Other trees and bushes include holm oaks and cedars, strawberry trees, so called on account of their round pinkish fruits, and winter flowering viburnums.

The gravelled shore is a fascinating place, very different from the soft clays and marshes on the other side of Southampton Water. It was formed a million years ago when the Solent coastline was beginning to assume the form we recognise today. In the place of the Solent a great river flowed from west to east. At times, when the ice caps melted, it flooded the estuaries of the streams which flowed into it, depositing gravels which the wind and tide cut into terraces. Among the shells which you will find in the gravel are slipper limpets, cockles, mussels, oysters, clams and periwinkles. The beach is also the home of a special kind of sea anemone which burrows under the gravel and reaches for food with its tentacles when the tide is in.

The Park is open all the year round but the chapel and tearooms open only from Easter to September. Ring the Park Office, 0703 455157, for details.

**Southampton (Solent Way):** From the earliest times Southampton has been a port and centre of shipbuilding benefiting from a deep and easy approach, double high tides and convenient access to the Continent. Inevitably this brought invaders. Saxon settlers built an important town, Hamwih, around AD 700 on the west bank of the Itchen. After the Conquest the Normans extended the town further west, built defences to the north, and brought increased trade and prosperity.

Throughout the Middle Ages Southampton merchants grew rich, especially in the wool and wine trades. When these declined, Southampton suffered hard times but in 1750 the town gained a new lease of life. Frederick, then Prince of Wales, bathed off the western shore, thoroughly enjoyed the experience, and returned several times bringing London society with him. A chalybeate spring was discovered and Southampton became a spa with all that entailed: fine houses for the rich, good coaching inns, assembly rooms and excellent shops.

The beginning of the 19th century saw the decline of the spa but the development of Southampton as a great port. Piers were constructed and new docks were built on reclaimed land. Southampton's greatest days as a passenger port began when it became the headquarters of the Royal Mail, Union Castle and Cunard steamship lines.

At the same time Southampton developed as a centre for commercial aviation. Supermarine Aviation Works at Woolston built the Empire class flying boats, operated by Imperial Airways and BOAC. Between the wars R.J. Mitchell, Supermarine's chief designer, worked on seaplanes to produce the Supermarine S6B which won the Schneider Trophy outright for Britain in 1931. Mitchell used the expertise he gained on seaplanes in his design for the Spitfire. But the developments in aviation led to changes which still affect Southampton today. In October 1958 Pan Am operated its new Boeing 707s on the New York-London route and the era of the great liners was over. Southampton is now one of our leading container ports.

**The Museum of Archaeology (Solent Way):** This museum tells the story of Southampton's three towns, Roman Clausentum, Saxon Hamwih and the medieval town, and displays illustrate the daily lives of their inhabitants. Entry is free and the museum is open every day except Monday.

**The Hall of Aviation (Solent Way):** The history of the development of aviation in the Solent is presented with displays of aircraft, models and plans. Pride of place is given to a spectacular Sandringham flying boat. The Hall also incorporates the R.J.

Mitchell memorial museum. The museum is open every day except Monday.

For more information about Southampton's museums, historic houses, guided walks, boat trips and other attractions contact the Tourist Information Centre, Above Bar (High Street Pedestrian Precinct), 0703 223855 ext. 615 or 0703 221106.

**Westwood Woodland Park:** The best way to enjoy the history and wildlife of this fascinating park is to take a guided walk with one of the Westwood Rangers. These are held every month and the Rangers also organise visits for local schools, clean-up days and volunteer days, a slide show, horseriding permits, special visits for groups, and many other events such as art walks and guided walks in French. For details contact the Westwood office, open normal office hours and most weekends, 0703 455157 ext. 25. To receive free information on Westwood you can join the mailing list.

Westwood is always open, and parking and entry are free.

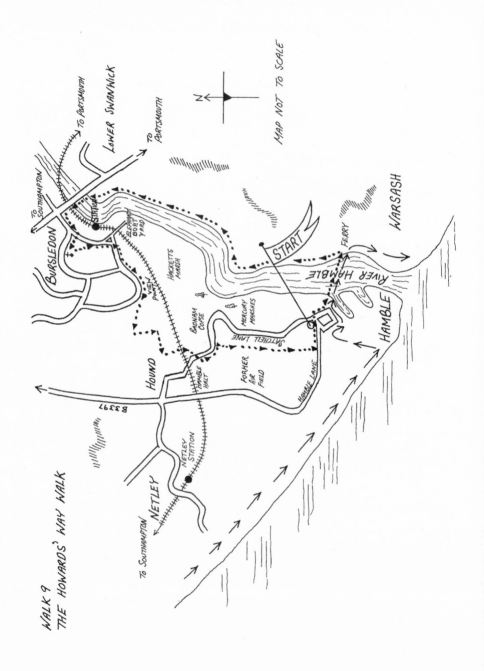

WALK 9
THE HOWARDS' WAY WALK

MAP NOT TO SCALE

N

TO PORTSMOUTH

LOWER SWANWICK

TO PORTSMOUTH

TO SOUTHAMPTON

BURSLEDON

STATION

ELEPHANT BOAT YARD

HACKETT'S MARSH

VIEW POINT

HOUND

BADNAM COPSE

MERCURY MARSHES

START

FERRY

WARSASH

RIVER HAMBLE

HAMBLE

SATCHELL LANE

HAMBLE HALT

FORMER AIR FIELD

HAMBLE LANE

B3397

NETLEY STATION

NETLEY

TO SOUTHAMPTON

# The *Howards' Way* walk –
# Hamble and Bursledon

(Solent Way – the Royal Victoria Country Park
to Warsash Ferry landing)

**Introduction:** The Solent Way glances only briefly at the Hamble
river, as, hugging the coastline, it crosses over to Warsash and
continues eastwards. But this historic river, world famous as a
yachting centre and still bordered in places with marshes and
ancient oak woods, richly repays a closer look. Some of the
scenery will be familiar if you watched the television series
*Howards' Way*, but that revealed only a small part of the river's
story.

The walk begins in Hamble village and after crossing the river by
ferry, leaves the Solent Way to follow the riverbank north to
Bursledon. Today this mainly 18th century village sleeps peacefully
on its wooded hillside, but in the past it was a hive of activity. Great
battleships were built in the creek below the church, including HMS
*Elephant*, Nelson's flagship at the battle of Copenhagen. Beside the
road, just past the village, there is a fine viewpoint overlooking the
whole river estuary to the Isle of Wight hills. Woodland paths lead
back to Hamble where you may wish to linger and perhaps take a trip
on the river.

**Distance:** The Royal Victoria Country Park to Warsash Ferry
landing on the Solent Way 2.5 miles. Circular walk 6.5 miles. OS
Landranger series 1:50 000 map 196 The Solent also OS Outdoor
Leisure series 1:25 000 map 22 New Forest.

**Refreshments:** Hamble is the thirsty walker's dream with five
pubs, three of which are close together near the waterfront. There are

WALK NINE

also restaurants and tearooms. Halfway round the walk there are
several pubs near the bridge at Bursledon and The Vine in Old
Bursledon. In the summer, Blue Star Boats have a refreshment kiosk
on Hamble foreshore.

**How to get there:** From Southampton, cross the Itchen Bridge
(toll), and take the A3025 for a little over 3 miles to its junction
with the B3397 (Hamble Lane). Turn right and drive to the car
park on the left in Hamble Square. Or exit from the M27 at
junction 8 and drive south following the signs for Hamble down
Hamble Lane. The car park is large and, at the time of writing,
free.

Citybus runs a service to Hamble from Southampton as does
Solent Blue Line, ring 0703 618233 for details. For times of County
Bus services ring 100 and ask for freephone County Bus.

The circular walk can be started from Bursledon station which is
on the main Southampton-Portsmouth line.

**Hamble Ferry:** At the time of writing the ferry has no fixed
schedule but runs on demand without fail weekdays 7 am to 5.45 pm,
Saturday 7 am to 4 pm, and Sunday 9 am to 4 pm. For further
information ring 0703 454512.

**Hamble river trips:** Blue Star Boats on the Hamble foreshore run
river trips daily and also offer self-drive motor dinghies on an hourly
or daily basis. Ring 0489 572840 for details.

**Solent Way – the Royal Victoria Country Park to Warsash Ferry
landing:** From the entrance to the Park continue along the shore
road, past the Hard, leaving the Royal Chapel on your left. Follow
the beach past the sailing club and dinghy park. A few yards further
on, a narrow path climbs Hamble Cliff and leads through trees above
the beach for a short distance which makes a pleasant alternative to
the shingle.

Follow the beach past the works of Aerostructures, where
aircraft components are manufactured including parts for the
Airbus jet. During the First World War Sir Edwin Alliott Verdon-
Roe established an aircraft factory here. His Avro 504N airplanes
became the standard training aircraft for the Royal Air Force

between the wars. He was the first Englishman to construct and fly his own airplane.

Stretching into Southampton Water ahead is the long jetty serving the huge BP oil terminal. A railway, still visible, used to run from the terminal to join the main line near Hamble Halt, crossing Hamble airfield on the way. One of the first lessons cadets being trained there had to learn was that aircraft gave way to trains!

As you approach the BP terminal you need to take a concrete pathway above the beach on the left to cross an inlet. When the fence around the terminal turns left keep straight on along the edge of Hamble Common. Pass the first footpath sign on the left, but turn left at the second post, just after you cross an embankment, the remains of settlements established by invaders from Gaul around 500 BC. Now a pleasant path through coppiced woodland and gorse takes you to a lane. Follow the lane, and when Copse Road bends away on the left, bear a little right up School Lane. Opposite the old school (now School House) follow the signs right and walk past Hamble Green with its attractive cottages and down narrow Ferryhill to the waterside. Follow the route of Walk Nine to catch the ferry across the river to Warsash landing. Now turn to Walk Ten.

**The Walk:** Turn left from the car park in Hamble Square and walk towards the top of the narrowest part of the High Street, which runs steeply down to the waterfront. To the left is Copperhill Terrace, a row of 18th century cottages, and overhanging the roadside opposite is the 17th century Old House, half-timbered and infilled with herringbone brickwork. The narrow street – only ten foot wide in places – turns at the end to bring you to the river, crowded with an extraordinary variety of yachts both sail and power.

Yachts built to the very latest design, ocean racers, old-timers and fishing boats are mirrored together in the still water against a background of woods and marshes. There is very little room for visiting boats as three yacht clubs are based here. The row of cottages adjacent to the quay and partly concealed by a magnificent magnolia are the headquarters of the Royal Southern Yacht Club which moved from Southampton in 1936. The river is also the home of the Royal Air Force Yacht Club and the Hamble River Sailing Club. Upstream is the first marina to be built in Britain,

Port Hamble, while beyond is Mercury marina, and downstream are the masts of another marina at Hamble Point.

Take the ferry from Hamble quay across the river to the raised footpath that runs over the marshes on the other side. Records show that a ferry was operating here as early as 1493. The walk now leaves the Solent Way and turns left to follow the east bank of the river upstream. The path crosses saltmarshes and mudlands interlaced with creeks, happy hunting grounds for waders especially redshank, dunlin and curlew. Rock pipits hop along the shoreline.

Inland are brackish lagoons, thick with reeds with here and there a watchful heron and perhaps a kingfisher. Known as 'Bunny Meadows' this land was once drained and reclaimed as grazing. The tide breached the banks in the 1930s and the fields reverted to mudland. Culverts in the present restored path preserve their inter-tidal character.

Across the river is another nature reserve, Mercury Marshes. It is named after TS *Mercury*, a training ship with a shore base, for boys wishing to join the Royal Navy and the Merchant Service. It was founded in 1885 on the Isle of Wight by Charles Hoare and at his death in 1908 the school was run for 42 years by the famous scholar and sportsman, C.B. Fry. Due to financial difficulties TS *Mercury* was forced to close in 1968. There is a memorial in the churchyard to ex-cadets who lost their lives in both world wars.

Follow the footpath, walk through Universal Shipyards, and join the footpath again just past the wooden office buildings. As you approach Swanwick the path rises to pass some houses and meet a tarmac lane. Keep straight on with the river still close on your left to pass the public Hard close to Moody's Shipyard and marina. Opposite the Hard is a row of tiny, very attractive cottages. Follow the lane – Swanwick Shore Road – to meet the main road, the A27. Turn left and walk along the path beside the road to cross the bridge over the river and go under the railway bridge. Almost immediately turn left along a lane following the sign for Bursledon station. When the road divides bear right up Church Lane, then left to the church of St Leonard with its small half-timbered tower and long wooden porch. The church was built by monks from Hamble Priory in the early 13th century. It is known as the shipbuilders' church and inside is a memorial to George Parsons who built HMS *Elephant*, Nelson's flagship.

Follow the narrow footpath that runs down the hill through the woods to the left of the church. Before the railway was built in 1881 causing the creek and foreshore to silt up, tidal waters lapped the foot of the hill.

When the path divides, take the right-hand path to a lane in Old Bursledon. Continue up the hill passing Greywell, the first of many elegant 18th century houses built of grey and red bricks from the local works. At the next junction our route bears right but first I suggest you should make a short detour down to the railway bridge directly ahead. From the bridge you can look down on the Elephant boatyard where of course the famous man-of-war was built along with many others throughout the 14th, 15th and 16th centuries. A little further down the road you will see the signboard of the Jolly Sailor pub – well worth a visit. In the past, as there were no good roads, the river was the main highway and sailing coasters lay off the Jolly Sailor to unload their cargoes on to lighters which went up river on the tide to Botley.

Return to the junction and follow Lands End Road through Old Bursledon. As the road rises with a hedge on your left look for a small wooden gate leading to a viewpoint. The landowner has made this and invites you to enter. Now there is a magnificent bird's eye view of the lower reaches of the river winding to the sea and the hills of the Isle of Wight. Below lies Hackett's Marsh, rich in rare plants and wildlife, especially insects. An information board indicates the outstanding features of the panorama before you.

Return to the road and keep straight on at the next junction down the High Street past the Old Cottage. Cross the top of Salterns Lane and follow Kew Lane for a few yards until it bends right. On the corner look for a narrow footpath on the left running close to the left-hand side of a house. Take this leafy path as it makes its way downhill to meet a lane by a footpath sign. Follow the lane until it bears right. Now keep straight on along the footpath ahead following the sign. Cross a lane and keep straight on over a stream bordered by kingcups and yellow irises to enter the ancient oak and beech woods of Badnam Copse.

Climb up through the trees, then bear left along the main track to follow a terraced path along the wooded hillside to meet a lane. Bear right along the lane for only a few yards and as you come to the edge of the wood, just before the lane turns right, look very carefully (no sign) for the beginning of a footpath on the left to the right of a wire fence. Cross to the footpath and follow it with the green tower of the Chapel of the Royal Victoria Country Park directly ahead. The path bends left and continues to take you over a railway bridge, to meet Satchell Lane. Bear left along the lane for a little over ¼ mile. The land on the right was once part of the airfield of the College of Air Training established at Hamble in 1960.

The lane bends sharply left and after about 30 yards look for a footpath on the right indicated by a prominent 'no cycling' symbol. Turn right and follow this, past a hangar. Keep straight on along the lane past Hamble House Gardens to meet the road opposite Hamble's priory church, a lovely Norman building.

In 1109 Benedictine monks from the Abbey of Tiron in France were granted land here by the Bishop of Winchester. They built a priory and the church of St Andrew dates from that time. The Hamble river was famous for its oysters and during the following centuries the Prior of Hamble would send in Lent 20,000 of these delectable shellfish to the monks of St Swithins in Winchester. In return the six monks at Hamble received 21 loaves and 42 flagons of ale each week.

Turn left along the High Street, past Ye Olde Whyte Harte pub dating from 1563, and the late 17th century gun house which has four cast iron guns partly buried in front of it. The car park is on your left.

### Historical Notes

**Hamble:** Hamble's advantages as a port have been recognised from earliest times. St Bede, writing in the 8th century, described its double high tides. The channel was deep enough for most vessels and well sheltered, and timber for shipbuilding was available locally.

Throughout the centuries, fishing was the most important industry. Hamble fishermen trawled for scallops off the coast of France, and manned a large fleet of spratters and later crabbers, bringing their catch from the West Country and southern Ireland. It was a dangerous occupation, and before a voyage the fishermen would pray for a safe return and make a cut on the church door. Those who returned would give thanks and make their mark into a cross. Those marks can still be seen.

Today, most of the fishing boats have given place to yachts but the skills of the seamen are as vital as ever. You will find every kind of specialist in Hamble's narrow lanes and along the waterfront: designers, builders, sailmakers, marine engineers, riggers and chandlers. Hamble has adapted to the times but not, I think, changed its character.

**Bursledon:** Surrounded by oak woods and situated beside a sheltered S-bend of the river, Bursledon was an ideal place for shipbuilding. The first man-of-war, *St George*, was launched there on St George's Day 1338 by King Edward III. The remains of Henry V's great warship, *Grace Dieu*, still lie at the bottom of the creek. She had been sent to Bursledon 'for the safe keeping' and either caught fire or was struck by lightning.

During the 17th century the Wyatt family controlled most shipbuilding, and the French wars resulted in many contracts for warships being placed by the Navy Board during the 18th and early 19th centuries.

Old Bursledon is a conservation area and has some beautiful old houses including the Dolphin, which has a 16th century porch, and an attractive cluster of almshouses with elaborate brickwork and chimneys.

**Hamble College of Air Training:** The college was established at Hamble in 1960 by BOAC and BEA together with the Department of Education to satisfy an increasing need for civilian pilots. There were no longer sufficient ex-military pilots available and the airline industry was booming. The college became famous for the excellence of its instruction and its cost-effectiveness. Cadets were trained using only piston-driven aircraft – single-engined Chipmunks, twin-engined Piper Apaches and later Cherokees and Barons – and jet simulators. The cadets graduated into the co-pilot's seat of one of the large passenger-carrying jet aircraft with 250 hours flying, then the minimum for a commercial pilot's licence. As aircraft grew larger and began to need only two-pilot crews instead of three, a surplus of pilots led to the closure of the college in 1984.

**Hamble Common (Solent Way):** From earliest times Hamble villagers have claimed their rights of common, grazing their cattle and cutting the gorse for fuel. As a result the common remains unimproved grassland and is a very special place, rich in wildlife, particularly butterflies and reptiles. In Tudor times it was fortified and St Andrew's Castle was built off the Spit in 1544. At low tide the foundations can still be seen. Iron Age peoples settled on the common but finds have proved that people were living there as early as 2000 BC. A circular walk has been devised around the common, leading past the beach where an anti-aircraft gun stands on a concrete emplacement. In 1939 guns stood here to protect Southampton Water. East of the footpath, on the Point, are the offices of Cougar Marine and the forest of masts of Hamble Point marina.

# A Solent wilderness – Hook-with-Warsash Nature Reserve

(Solent Way – Warsash Ferry landing to Solent Breezes Caravan Park)

**Introduction:** Richly contrasting scenery makes this short circular walk a really special experience. Almost all the walk is in the Hook-with-Warsash Nature Reserve which covers a large area of amazingly varied countryside. From the shingle banks beside Southampton Water paths lead over reclaimed pasture, by shallow lagoons and freshwater lakes fringed with rushes to return to the waterside through beautiful oak and beech woods.

Throughout the year this variety of habitats provides homes for a wealth of wildlife including oyster-catchers and curlews along the shore, kingfishers, warblers and herons around the freshwater lakes, and in the woods, woodpeckers, nuthatches and blackcaps. Rabbits scamper among the gorse bushes and large holes in the soft earth bordering the lanes betray the presence of foxes and badgers. In May and June the wild flowers are at their loveliest. The marshy areas are golden with kingcups and the woods full of bluebells.

**Distance:** Warsash Ferry landing to Solent Breezes Caravan Park on the Solent Way 2.5 miles. Circular walk 4 miles. OS Landranger series 1:50 000 map 196 The Solent.

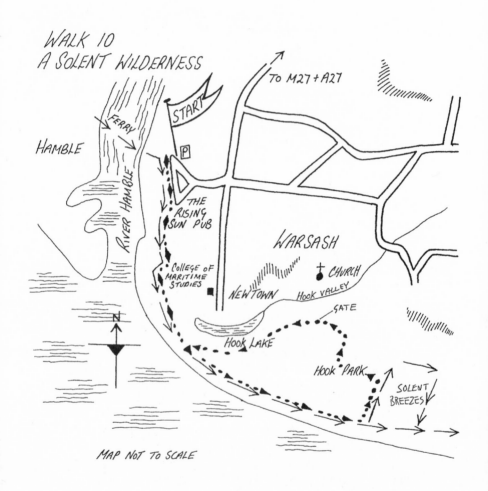

WALK 10
A SOLENT WILDERNESS

HAMBLE

FERRY

START

TO M27 + A27

P

THE RISING SUN PUB

River Hamble

College of MARITIME STUDIES

WARSASH

NEWTOWN

Hook VALLEY

CHURCH

N

Hook LAKE

GATE

Hook PARK

SOLENT BREEZES

MAP NOT TO SCALE

**Refreshments:** The Rising Sun, Warsash, has a lovely view of the river. Restaurants at Warsash include Edwardo's Cortigo (formerly the Crab and Lobster) and Le Bon Viveur.

**How to get there:** The walk starts from the free car park on the corner of Shore Road and Passage Lane, close to Warsash waterfront. The best approach to Warsash is to exit from the M27 at junction 8. At the roundabout take the first road on the left, the A27 for Fareham. Cross the Hamble river at Bursledon, continue to Sarisbury and turn right down Barnes Lane before the church for Warsash. At a junction, bear right down Brook Lane. At the next roundabout (opposite the Great Harry pub) turn right down Shore Road following the one-way system. This curves right to bring you to Warsash waterfront. Ignore the car park on the left (there is a four hour limit and you may want longer) and keep on round the corner where there is a large free car park immediately on your left. The walk starts from here; it can also be started from Warsash village, served by buses from Gosport, Bursledon and Southampton.

**Solent Way – Warsash Ferry landing to Solent Breezes Caravan Park:** From the ferry landing on the Warsash shore turn right and follow the riverside path towards Warsash village. The path leads to a car park on your left. Now follow the route of Walk Ten as far as Solent Breezes Caravan Park. Then turn to Walk Eleven.

**The Walk:** Turn right from the car park entrance and follow Shore Road along the Warsash waterfront, past the Sailing Club to the car park beside the pier in front of the Rising Sun pub. A D-Day memorial in the corner of the car park commemorates the departure of British and Allied naval and commando units from the Hamble river, on the night of 5th June 1944 for the Normandy beaches. Three thousand commandos embarked in 36 landing craft of HMS *Tormentor* based nearby. A plaque on the wall of the Rising Sun also commemorates the occasion.

Pass the Rising Sun on your left and take the shore path ahead to the right of the Warsash Sailing Club's private road. On the wall of the club and on the gate is a drawing of a large lobster. Warsash was famous until after the Second World War for its crab and lobster teas.

The path rises to follow the top of a grassy embankment studded with old oak trees. It is said that smugglers found these trees useful for concealing contraband. The WI publication *It Happened in Hampshire* gives an amusing explanation of the name of the village. Evidently, in papers relating to Titchfield Abbey, Warsash is called Warish-asse-feld on account of the donkeys feeding on the embankment.

Dropping down to the shore again, the path passes part of the buildings of Warsash College of Maritime Studies (formerly School of Navigation). At the end of the college's long jetty, lifeboats and liferafts are poised ready for the cadets to practise lowering and boarding. Past the college, the path bears right to go over the sluice gates and dam across the Hook channel. Until the dam was put across at the end of the 18th century the Hook river provided a haven for shipping and had shipbuilding and repair yards. Now, in their place, lagoons and grasslands stretch inland towards freshwater lakes and vast reedbeds.

Ahead a shingle spit curls round the coast to form a hook at the mouth of the Hamble river. The spit supports many interesting plants including sea rocket with its clusters of tiny lilac-coloured flowers, yellow horned poppy and the striped pink and white bells of sea bindweed.

Follow the path as it bears left beside the shore, past an old gun emplacement. Through a fringe of tamarisk bushes on your left a path runs inland beside a lake fringed with rushes. This is our return route. Continue along the shingle past an area of rough grassland on your left, Hook Links. This is the site of a Roman saltworks where Roman saltworkers' artefacts have been found. A narrow creek meanders across the links lined with bulrushes and sedges.

The path continues past dense masses of gorse and hawthorn noisy with scolding stonechats. In autumn you may be lucky enough to see the dainty long-tailed Dartford warbler here.

Follow the beach until you come to Solent Breezes Caravan Park. Just before this site, turn left along the lane, with the site on your right. This is Workman's Lane, a name recalling a factory which stood here a hundred years ago. The factory manufactured alkali by distilling wood ash. A by-product was charcoal which was used to smelt iron. Portland cement was also produced here by mixing chalk and mud. Now the fields leading down to the shore on your right are a bird sanctuary.

When the lane bears right the walk leaves the Solent Way. Keep straight on following the footpath sign over a stile. Continue straight on and then follow Workman's Lane as it bears left to a T-junction. Turn right and follow the gravel track for about ¼ mile. Look carefully for a good footpath leading down into woodland on your left (no footpath sign). You will see a wooden gate a short way down the path. Turn left and follow the path to the gate. Careful navigation is needed here! **Do not go through the gate**. Bear a little left and you will see two possible paths ahead. Follow the right-hand path as it becomes a terraced way along the side of a steep valley. (This is a public right of way though unmarked on the OS Pathfinder map.)

The path through Hook Valley is beautiful. Deep in the valley is a dense jungle of alder and willow rising to slopes covered with birch, ash, elm, maple and holly. Oak and beech trees shade your path along the lip of the valley. All kinds of woodland birds and plants can find a home in this unspoilt wilderness so close to the crowded Solent shore.

Leave the woods past a barrier and continue down a lane to a road. Cross the road and follow the footpath sign straight ahead. Climb the stile and keep on along the footpath beside the dense reed beds which fill Hook Lake. (If this is muddy, you can walk through the reeds.) These thickets give cover for many birds that enjoy freshwater, including kingfishers, reed and sedge warblers, little grebes and herons.

The path joins your original path close to Hook Spit by the concrete gun emplacement. Once again you have wide views of Southampton Water. Turn right and retrace your steps over the dam back to Warsash and along the waterfront to the car park. Before you leave, you might like to rest for a while on one of the seats thoughtfully placed close by and enjoy the view of the Hamble river.

## Historical Notes

**Hook-with-Warsash Nature Reserve:** This is one of the most fascinating of Hampshire County Council's reserves as the countryside is so varied. And most of it is a real wilderness. Possibly it is quieter today than at any time in its history. Before the Hook river was dammed it was the harbour for Newtown, a settlement on its north bank, south of Warsash. Shipbuilding and repairing evidently flourished on the river making it a larger port than Hamble at that time. Pitchponds Road in Newtown recalls those days. And it is interesting to note that when Edward III mustered transport to convey his army to France in 1345 Hook provided 11 ships and 208 mariners and Hamble only 7 ships and 117 mariners. Portsmouth only contributed 5 ships and 96 mariners.

Though the harbour was still in use in 1600 it is possible it began to silt up. But the damming of the estuary by William Hornby at the end of the 18th century put an end to the river's usefulness. Hornby retired from his position as Governor of Bombay in 1803 at the age of 30. So impressed was he with his official residence that he built a replica of Government House, Bombay, at Hook. Fitting parkland must surround it so he dammed the river to make a lake and destroyed a village. The house was burnt down but much of Hook Park remains, forming part of the nature reserve.

**Warsash:** The row of sturdy cottages leading down to the Rising Sun on the waterfront at Warsash still conveys the atmosphere of the days when the village was a small fishing community, noted for its crabs and lobsters. The fishermen in their specially constructed 'crabbers' brought them from Brittany, Ireland and the West Country to be stored in tanks at Warsash before being distributed inland.

Later it was discovered that the stony soil surrounding the village was excellent for growing strawberries. School holidays were adjusted to match the pressure of work in the fields when all hands were needed for 'strawing down' and picking. Some of the strawberry fields have been built over but there is still plenty of good fruit to be bought by the roadside in the season.

Today, yachting is important at Warsash but the waterfront presents a less crowded scene than Hamble. A striking feature is a large black and white tower, the offices of the harbour master who, with the County Council, is responsible for the river. Close by are the premises of Warsash Sailing Club and the Solent School of Yachting.

**Warsash College of Maritime Studies:** The buildings of the college occupy a commanding position at the mouth of the Hamble, a fitting position for a college famed internationally for training merchant navy officers. The college was established in 1935 by Captain G.W. Wakeford and moved into its present buildings in 1946. Its excellent equipment includes a bridge simulator.

Sail training is still an important part of a cadet's course and some keep their own small boats. Ashlett creek, on the other side of the water, is a favourite destination.

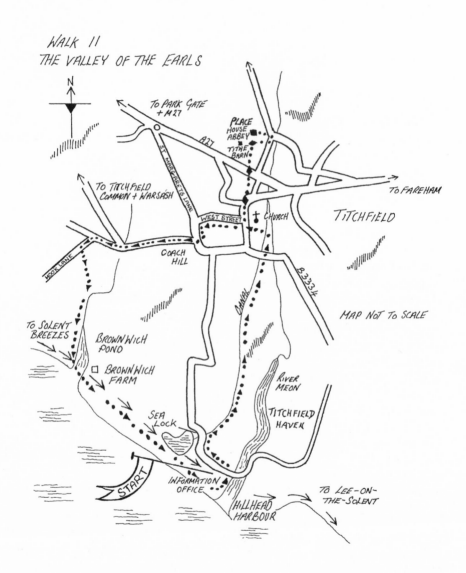

WALK II
THE VALLEY OF THE EARLS

N

TO PARK GATE
+ M 27

PLACE
HOUSE
ABBEY

TITHE
BARN

ST. MARGARET'S LANE

A27

TO TITCHFIELD
COMMON + WARSASH

WEST STREET

✝ CHURCH

TITCHFIELD

TO FAREHAM

COACH
HILL

HOOK LANE

CANAL

B3334

MAP NOT TO SCALE

TO SOLENT
BREEZES

BROWNWICH
POND

BROWNWICH
FARM

RIVER
MEON

SEA
LOCK

TITCHFIELD
HAVEN

START

INFORMATION
OFFICE

HILLHEAD
HARBOUR

TO LEE-ON-
THE-SOLENT

# The valley of the earls – Titchfield village, canal and Abbey ruins

## (Solent Way – Solent Breezes Caravan Park to Titchfield Haven, Meon Shore)

**Introduction:** There will be something to interest everyone in this superb ramble of a little over 6 miles. The walk starts by following a canal-side path overlooking Titchfield Haven Nature Reserve and leading to Titchfield village beside the Meon river. Today, this charming cluster of mainly half-timbered and Georgian houses could not look more peaceful but once it was a busy port. And every year, on the last Monday in October, the villagers remember the year 1611 when their landlord, the third Earl of Southampton, blocked the mouth of the Meon and put an end to their trade. A day-long carnival is held culminating in the lighting of a huge bonfire on the recreation ground.

Shakespeare knew Titchfield. The third Earl was his patron and there is a tradition that some of his plays were acted here. If you follow an optional walk of about a mile you can visit Place House, the remains of a Tudor mansion built by the first Earl of Southampton from the ruins of a 13th century Abbey, and the magnificent tithe barn close by where it is said *Romeo and Juliet* was first performed.

The return route brings us back to the present day. The path follows one of the woodland walks established recently by Hampshire County Council in the Brownwich valley. This is a modern success story. Here you can see careful wildlife conservation co-existing happily with productive farming. And to finish, there is a clifftop walk with splendid Solent views.

**Distance:** Solent Breezes Caravan Park to Titchfield Haven, Meon Shore, on the Solent Way 2 miles (2.5 miles by longer route). Circular walk 6 miles. Optional extra mile to visit Place House. OS Landranger series 1:50 000 map 196 The Solent.

**Refreshments:** All facilities and pubs in Titchfield village including a bakery. The garden centre at Place House has a coffee shop, and on the Solent Way there is a refreshment kiosk in Solent Breezes Caravan Park.

**How to get there:** The walk starts from the large parking area of Titchfield Haven, Meon Shore. Leave the M27 at junction 9 (Fareham West) to follow the A27. At the first roundabout continue along the A27 in the direction of Titchfield for a little over a mile to the next roundabout. Here, you leave the A27 and take the third exit, St Margaret's Lane. In about ½ mile you come to a T-junction, Coach Hill. Turn left for only a few yards, then right down Posbrook Lane signposted Meon. This becomes Triangle Lane and leads towards the coast, turning sharply left over a canal bridge to the parking area on the right overlooking the beach.

**Solent Way – Solent Breezes Caravan Park to Titchfield Haven, Meon Shore:** At present there are two possible routes past Solent Breezes Caravan Park. Walkers are welcome to cross the park itself. Follow the beach to a flight of steps on your left leading up the cliff into the caravan park. Keep straight ahead for a few yards, then turn right past the pub. The site office is on your left. Walk through the park to cross a stile by a footpath sign on the clifftop.

However, the cliff edge is unstable and a new, much longer route round the park has been signposted. Just before the park, turn left up the lane following the route of Walk Ten. When the lane bears right, leave the route of Walk Ten, which continues straight on over a stile, and follow the lane until a sign on your right indicates a path which eventually leads you back to the cliff again on the other side of Solent Breezes Caravan Park.

Continue along the clifftop path, with splendid Solent views, to descend into the shallow valley of the Brownwich stream. Walk on to Titchfield Haven car park on the Meon Shore tracing the final part of Walk Eleven (see p. 99).

**The Walk:** The long parking area close to the Meon Shore is beside the road which runs along the seaward side of the Titchfield Haven Nature Reserve. Cross the road and climb the stile which leads to the entrance to the reserve. (It is near a prominent sea mark.) Do not enter the reserve, but turn immediately left and follow a narrow path which soon bears right beside a stream. The road is on the left. As the road curves sharply left to cross the canal, turn left along a small gravel path to cross a stile to the canal bank. At this point, the canal flows gently through its original sea lock completed in 1611 as part of the Earl of Southampton's plan to divert water from the river Meon and drain the estuary. As a navigable channel the canal was a failure, but today the towpath provides a wonderful walk.

Follow the path beside the canal, at first shaded by oak trees and later across water meadows. The more invasive plants have been cut back and the canal flows freely over waving fans of weed between masses of water-loving flowers including marsh marigolds, purple loosestrife and flowering rushes. On your right you have a good view over the lagoons and reed beds of Titchfield Haven Nature Reserve. A recent addition to the wealth of wildlife to be seen here is a colony of Cetti's warblers.

The path continues for about 2 miles to Titchfield village. Cross a minor road and continue straight on beside the water to a small bridge on your left leading to the old church of St Peter. In the days when Titchfield was a flourishing port on a wide estuary, there were wharves close by where once barges unloaded stone from the Isle of Wight, Charles I embarked for Carisbrooke and Huguenot refugees landed to seek new homes.

Turn left to cross the bridge and walk through the churchyard. St Peter's, with its early Anglo-Saxon porch and chapel housing the 16th century monument to the second Earl of Southampton and his parents, is one of Hampshire's finest village churches.

From the church walk down Church Street, lined with attractive Georgian and half-timbered houses, to the High Street. Now you have a choice of routes. The shorter walk, about 6 miles, continues straight across the High Street and up West Street. But if you would like to visit Place House, adding an extra mile to the walk, you can make a detour here.

For the longer walk, turn right through the village. At a road junction bear right for only a few yards. Do not follow East Street which now turns sharply right, but keep straight on past the half-timbered entrance to the Old Lodge. Follow the narrow alley ahead and then the footpath with a wall on your left. Cross the A27 and climb the stile directly ahead leading to a footpath. (The gap at the side of the stile is barred with barbed wire.) You will see the remains of Place House – the magnificent gatehouse – ahead, a little to your right, and as you follow the path, the former Abbey's huge tithe barn on your left. The barn is open every day (including Sunday morning) selling fresh produce, and a visit is a must! Over 500 years old, 157 feet long and 46 feet wide, it is one of the finest timber-framed structures in Hampshire. The main vertical posts are whole trees turned upside down.

A few yards past the barn, turn right past the greenhouses of the garden centre to the road. Turn left and on your left is the entrance to Place House, now in the care of English Heritage. Through the arch you can see the imposing gatehouse, distinguished by four octagonal towers. This is almost all that remains of a Tudor mansion built by Thomas Wriothesley, later first Earl of Southampton, using the stonework of the Abbey established here in 1232 and dissolved in 1537. Among the many visitors to Place House was William Shakespeare.

Retrace your steps to Titchfield village and the corner of West Street where you rejoin the route of the shorter walk. Follow West Street to the top of the hill where it meets St Margaret's Lane. Turn left to walk to the road to Titchfield Common and Warsash. Turn right to follow this road to a T-junction where you bear left still following the Warsash Road. After about 100 yards turn left down Hook Lane. Shortly you will see the entrance to Hook Lane car park on your left and the start of a path along the Brownwich valley leading back to the coast.

Turn left, cross the car park, and beyond the fields ahead you will see the silver line of the Solent backed by the dark curve of the Isle of Wight hills. Follow the path as it brings you closer to the woods bordering the Brownwich stream. Under the County Council's ownership and management this has become a fascinating area. Within a farming environment, wildlife has been encouraged by planting and strengthening hedgerows and restoring and protecting grassy headlands, verges, ponds and meadows. Now skylarks and other ground-nesting birds have returned along with grasshoppers, butterflies and many small mammals.

The path leads through the fringes of the trees and along the western side of Brownwich Pond. Just past the pond turn left over a stile beside a gate to follow a path along the dam forming the southern bank. The pond is used for irrigation and fishing but it is also beautiful. In summer there are masses of water lilies.

When you come to a gate, turn right down some steps and follow a narrow path shaded by oak trees beside the Brownwich stream. The path turns right to cross a bridge over the stream and then bears left to emerge on the beach. Beside you, the stream trickles in a leisurely fashion through the shingle to meet the sea. **Solent Way walkers join here.** Turn left along the beach and after a few yards you will see a path climbing to the clifftop. Take this and follow the path back to the parking area at Titchfield Haven on the Meon Shore with marvellous views east and west over the Solent.

## Historical Notes

**Titchfield Haven Nature Reserve:** After the construction of a sea wall and one-way tidal flaps across the estuary of the Meon river in 1611, the area developed into a rich and varied freshwater marsh. This includes wet meadows, dense reedbeds, lagoons and a canal. As it is so close to the sea, in addition to nesting and resident species the Haven has become a refuge and a feeding area for vast numbers of migrant birds, especially during the winter months. It is also a sanctuary for animals including roe deer, foxes and badgers. Five hides easily reached by made-up paths and boardwalks have been constructed within the reserve to enable visitors to enjoy excellent views of the wildlife.

If you would like to visit the reserve you need a permit. Book in advance by applying to: The Naturalist Warden, Haven Cottage, Cliff Road, Hill Head, Fareham, Hants or telephone 0329 662145. You will be able to join one of the guided tours which lead from the reserve's information centre at 9.30 am and 1.30 pm on Fridays, Saturdays and Sundays. The centre is close to the car park on the Meon Shore. Follow the road in the direction of Hill Head harbour for a few yards and the centre is on your left.

**Titchfield village:** Titchfield is as charming as its name suggests. The narrow streets lined with homely houses, many half-timbered behind their Georgian façades, have succeeded in retaining their individuality and old-world atmosphere. The 20th century rushes past on the A27 while Titchfield remains an oasis of calm!

The church is Titchfield's greatest treasure and the residents care for it beautifully. Apart from the Saxon features and the Southampton monument I mentioned, a magnificently carved Norman arch leads from the western porch to the nave.

**Titchfield Abbey, Place House and Tithe Barn:** The Abbey was a house of Premonstratensian Canons who took their name from the monastery of Prémontré in France. For 300 years it was the centre of life at the head of the Meon Estuary and many royal visitors were entertained there. Richard II nearly drowned in one of the fishponds! Close by you can see the little bridge over the Meon built for Margaret of Anjou when she came to the Abbey to marry Henry VI. Among her wedding presents was a live lion.

After the Dissolution, the Abbey was remodelled as a stately home by Thomas Wriothesley, but some indication of its size can be obtained from lines marked on the ground. Among the remaining ruins is the entrance to the old chapter house and part of the cloister retaining its 13th century tiles.

Thomas Wriothesley finished building Place House (then called Palace House) in 1542. The imposing gatehouse which survives today was built across the nave of the church and retains the original doors. Later, Wriothesley was created Earl of Southampton. His grandson was Shakespeare's patron, the third Earl. But by 1741, the line had died out and the house was sold to the Delmé family who demolished most of the building, using the stone to build Cams Hall beside Fareham Creek. The ruins of Place House are open from Good Friday to September 30th, 10 am to 1 pm and 2 pm to 6 pm.

Don't miss a visit to the Tithe Barn! It is open every day and offers a splendid selection of farm produce and mouth-watering home-made cakes.

# A pageant of history –
# Spice Island and Southsea

(Solent Way – Titchfield Haven, Meon Shore, to Southsea Castle)

**Introduction:** Spice Island, the ramparts of Old Portsmouth, Southsea Castle and the D-Day Museum are some of the highlights of this walk. And as the route follows the coast along the sea-facing shore of Portsmouth Harbour there are wonderful views towards the Isle of Wight over the deep channel leading to Spithead where, for many centuries, the British fleet has assembled. We walk in the footsteps of many heroes: some born to command like Nelson, others of more humble origin like John Pounds, the crippled Portsmouth shoemaker, whose work for street urchins led to the establishment of 'Ragged Schools'.

The walk begins at Spice Island, the name given to Point, a small peninsula between a natural inlet, the Camber, and the entrance to Portsmouth Harbour. In the past it was outside the city limits and the jurisdiction of the magistrates, so became a favourite place for sailors to row ashore and relax. They were well able to do so as the close-packed area was famed for its hospitality, containing over 40 alehouses and inns. Today, times may have changed, but Spice Island, with its fishing boats unloading their catch on the medieval dock beside the Camber, retains its village atmosphere.

After following Old Portmouth's defences to Southsea Castle, there is a complete contrast. The walk leaves the Solent Way to cross Southsea Common and return past some of Southsea's elegant terraces, reminiscent of Bath, designed by a brilliant architect, Thomas Ellis Owen. And like Spice Island, Southsea retains its individuality. Even today, many older residents still refer to it as 'the village'.

WALK 12
A PAGEANT OF HISTORY

PORTSMOUTH

TO M275 + M27

TO DOCKYARD

PORTSMOUTH HARBOUR

GOSPORT

FERRY

STATION

SPICE — THE CAMBER ISLAND

RAMPARTS

GRAND PARADE

START

A3

CATHEDRAL

HIGH STREET

OLD PORTSMOUTH GARRISON CHURCH

KING'S BASTION

PIER ROAD

SOUTHSEA

QUEEN'S CRESCENT

ST JUDES CHURCH

KENT ROAD

SUSSEX ROAD

PORTLAND ROAD

PALMERSTON ROAD

CASTLE AVENUE

SOUTHSEA COMMON

D-DAY MUSEUM

SOUTHSEA CASTLE

N

MAP NOT TO SCALE

**Distance:** Titchfield Haven to Southsea Castle on the Solent Way 10 miles (including ferry from Gosport to Portsmouth harbour). Circular walk 4 miles. OS Landranger series 1:50 000 map 196 The Solent.

**Refreshments:** On the Solent Way there are refreshment facilities in the dockyard close to the Historic Ships. On Spice Island there are three pubs with good views, the Still and Western, the Spice Islander and the Lone Yachtsman. There are more good pubs and restaurants in Old Portsmouth and Southsea. Most retain their cosy Victorian atmosphere. There are cafés along Southsea sea front.

**How to get there:** Approaching Portsmouth from the M27, at junction 12 take the M275 and follow the signs for Old Portsmouth. At the first roundabout keep on along the A3. Do not turn for the Historic Ships but keep on the A3 which takes you down Old Portsmouth High Street, past Old Portsmouth Cathedral. Just before the road bears right in front of the ramparts turn left into the parking area in Grand Parade.

There is a regular service of buses and trains to Portsmouth Harbour. It is a little over ½ mile to the start of the walk. From the Hard, turn right into St George's Road, then in less than ¼ mile, turn right again into Gunwharf Road which leads you to Old Portsmouth High Street. Grand Parade leads off the other side of the road a little to your right.

**Museums:** Portsmouth City has some excellent museums apart from those mentioned. For details ring 0705 827261 or contact the Tourist Offices near Portsmouth Hard, 0705 826722, or near Southsea Castle, 0705 832464.

**Boat trips:** Blue Boat trips around Portsmouth Harbour. Ring 0705 822584 for details. Wight Line cruises to the Isle of Wight, round the harbour and the Beaulieu river, ring 0783 64602 for details. Also M and K Cruises, ring 0705 818155 for details. Trips leave from Clarence Pier.

**Solent Way – Titchfield Haven to Southsea Castle:**
Continue east along the promenade beside the Meon Shore past

103

Titchfield Haven Nature Reserve and around Hillhead Harbour. The Way leaves the road, keeping straight on over the car park to follow the sea wall and beach past Hill Head village.

Approaching Lee-on-the-Solent a slight deviation left then right, back to the beach, takes you across the Naval hovercraft slipway serving HMS *Daedalus*, the Fleet Air Arm's training establishment. You may see a flag with a red diamond on a white background flying from the Air Traffic Control building. This indicates that pilots are practising deck landings.

The Way continues along Lee-on-the-Solent sea front as far as a dinghy park. A short detour is necessary here. Turn left for a few yards, then right to the corner of Portsmouth Road at the most westerly point of the bare expanse of Browndown. Turn right, back to the shore, then left to follow the beach round Browndown, or if you prefer to avoid walking in heavy shingle continue along the Portsmouth Road, turn right into Browndown Road, then right at the roundabout to return to the beach close to Stokes Bay Road.

Both routes meet near a large 18th century gun battery which was used throughout both world wars. The grey house close by is Bay House, once a quiet retreat for Thomas Carlyle and later Edward VII.

Follow the coast to the high earth embankments surrounding Fort Gilkicker, one of the ring of forts strengthened by Lord Palmerston in the mid 19th century to protect Portsmouth Harbour. For a splendid view of Spithead, Ryde on the Isle of Wight, and the western Solent climb to the top of the embankments. Walk round the seaward side of the fort, then turn left to follow a path over the golf course (lake on your right).

At the T-junction turn right into Fort Road. A triangular stone column stands at the entrance to Fort Monkton, constructed in 1925 by Royal Engineer apprentices. Fork left here, then right down Haslar Road, past the famous Royal Naval Hospital. On the corner, as the road bears left, you pass the entrance to HMS *Dolphin*, which houses the Royal Navy Submarine Museum and HMS *Alliance*.

Turn right to cross Haslar Bridge, then bear a little right to follow a very pleasant footpath which leads along the Gosport Lines, ramparts designed by Sir Bernard de Gomme in 1660 (work proceeded slowly as there was a shortage of wheelbarrows). This leads to the ferry terminal.

Take the ferry to Portsmouth Hard. Walk up the road from the ferry landing and bear slightly right to walk to the left of the railway to the main road, Ordnance Road. Turn right, then right again under the bridge. Bear right beside the high walls of HMS *Vernon* and follow the wall as it leads right, past the gates of HMS *Nelson*. Cross the entrance to the Isle of Wight ferry and keep straight on down White Hart Road. Cross the road at the end and climb the ramparts ahead. Turn left to walk past the Square Tower and follow the route of Walk Twelve (p. 107) as far as Southsea Castle. Then turn to Walk Thirteen.

**The Walk:** The Grand Parade, where this walk starts, was the heart of Fortress Portsmouth, the military town. It was the scene of all ceremonial occasions and the centre of all the town's social activities. These will have been witnessed by the few colour-washed Georgian and Regency houses you will see beside the Square, survivors of the devastating air raids Portsmouth suffered during the last war.

With the old houses on your left, walk towards the area enclosed by a chain fence on your right. Outlined is the plan of the Garrison's guard house from which sentries were posted. Just past the enclosure turn right and walk up onto the ramparts, a magnificent sequence of gun batteries and towers, which formed Old Portsmouth's sea defences. You are standing on the Saluting Platform with a splendid view.

Ahead you look across the deep channel where for centuries British warships have anchored at Spithead, to Bembridge and Ryde on the Isle of Wight. Looking west, you can trace the line of ramparts leading to the Round Tower on Point, nicknamed Spice Island, at the entrance to Portsmouth Harbour. The Round Tower was the first permanent defensive building in Portsmouth built by order of Henry V. The entrance to the harbour was protected by a 'mightie chain of yron' which stretched across to a similar tower, Fort Blockhouse, on the Gosport shore. The site is now HMS *Dolphin*, the submarine establishment. The grey walls of Gosport's old defences lead to Haslar Royal Naval Hospital with its prominent water tower. And eastwards, protecting Spithead, are four forts built in the sea by order of Lord Palmerston in the middle of the 19th century, Spitbank, Horse Sands, No Man's Land and St Helens.

Turn right and follow the ramparts to the Square Tower built in 1494 by Henry VII with thick walls to resist cannon fire. Bear right round the tower to follow the gun battery platform towards the Round Tower. At its foot the waves break on the narrow shingle beach where in the past the sailors would draw up their boats and armies embark. Today the beach, known as 'hot walls', is a favourite spot for sunbathers.

Continue into the outer structure of the Round Tower, turn immediately left through the arches, then bear right to cross into the Round Tower itself. Climb the steps to the roof for more wide views. Return down the steps and back towards the arches where you will see a flight of steps leading down to street level. Descend the steps and walk towards the main street, Broad Street, which runs to the Hard at the end of Spice Island. The large boulder on your right commemorates the courage of two sailors who, using it as a shield, held at bay an enemy attack until their ship was safe.

You are now entering Spice Island. Until well into the 19th century we would be taking our courage into both hands! Today, it appears peaceful enough but the scenes of the past can easily be imagined. Turn left down Broad Street for only a few yards before turning left again down a narrow entry with Capstan House on your right. Now an old cobbled street, Tower Street, leads right between some 17th century cottages and the Captain's House where the marine artist William Wylie painted his famous *Battle of Trafalgar* scene.

Follow the next street bearing a little left to Bath Square. Quebec House on your left is the original bath house and the bathing cubicles remain beneath the building. Pass the Old Customs Watch House to the site of the former fish market beside the public Hard on the end of Spice Island.

This is overlooked by its three remaining pubs, the Still and Western (named after the bo's'n piping 'the still') and the Spice Islander which incorporates the Coal Exchange (coals were brought here from Newcastle), and the Lone Yachtsman named in honour of Sir Alec Rose. Now you have another fine view, this time of Portsmouth Harbour and HM Naval dockyard. The masts of HMS *Victory* rise behind the iron-clad hull of HMS *Warrior*. All kinds of ships pass close to Spice Island, from modern warships in their uniform grey and cross-channel ferries, to the colourful little fishing boats chugging in and out of the Camber.

Turn right to follow Broad Street until you come to a road called Seager's Court on your left. It is worth making a detour here to capture the fishing village atmosphere of Spice Island. At the end of the road you come to the Camber, a busy scene with small boats rocking gently in the small natural harbour.

Retrace your steps and follow Broad Street in the direction of the Square Tower. You pass the site of St James's gate, built in 1687, which behind a moat and drawbridge separated Spice Island from the mainland. The gate was removed in 1860. At the foot of Old Portsmouth High Street, the Sally Port opens through the defences to the beach. A plaque reads 'From this place naval heroes innumerable have embarked to fight their country's battles'. The granite knot close by commemorates the sailing from Spithead of the first fleet carrying settlers to Australia.

Climb the steps to the ramparts to the left of the Square Tower and turn left to follow the defences. **Solent Way joins here.** Cross the Saluting Platform and continue along the outer wall with the moat and Long Curtain on your left. These are part of the once extensive fortifications designed by Sir Bernard De Gomme by order of Charles II to counter threats by the Dutch fleet.

The walk continues by the sea for a mile to Southsea Castle with the wide green expanse of Southsea Common on your left. Clarence Pier was built in 1861 to serve the Isle of Wight steamers. Earlier in the century, as Southsea developed as a fashionable resort, it was the site of a pump room, baths and reading room.

Just before you come to the Sea Life Centre, bear right to the sea wall. Leaving the Sea Life Centre on your left, follow the sea front to Southsea Castle. Built by Henry VIII in 1544, at a point where the deepwater channel brought ships close to the shore and in range of its guns, this impressive, grey stone building has been an active military fortress for over 400 years but has never fired a shot in anger.

Some rare birds visit the rocks below Southsea Castle, notably in recent years a few purple sandpipers. The walk now turns inland. Just past the castle, turn left up some stone steps, then left again to walk down to the road leading to the castle entrance. Follow the road away from the castle to the main road. On your left is the D-Day Museum with its distinctive circular building housing the splendid Operation Overlord Embroidery. Keep straight on down Castle Avenue, over Clarence Parade and down Palmerston Road. In front of the pedestrian precinct, turn left for just a few yards, then right into Portland Road. Immediately on your right is Portland Terrace, a beautiful crescent of Regency styled houses designed by Thomas Ellis Owen in 1846. His own house, Dovercourt, now part of Portsmouth High School, stands opposite on the corner of Kent Road.

To see more of Owen's houses, turn right into Kent Road, then just before St Jude's church – designed and paid for by Owen and dedicated to the patron saint of hopeless cases – turn left down Queen's Grove leading to Queen's Crescent. Bear left here past the large Victorian houses, once almost entirely military and naval enclosures, then turn right into Sussex Road. A narrow carriage drive curves in front of another terrace designed by Owen, with deep arched doorways and delicate wrought-iron balconies. At the end of Sussex Road turn left to rejoin Kent Road.

Turn right towards the common which you will see ahead. Cross Kent Road and follow the footpath which runs diagonally over the common towards Clarence Pier. Halfway you come to Duisberg Way. Turn right to walk to Pier Road. Bear left along Pier Road for just a few yards and look for a footpath on the right, leading towards Lord Nelson's statue. Turn right to follow the footpath over the green which was once the garrison's recreation ground. Nelson stands looking seawards and the inscription reminds us he spent some of his last hours at the George in Old Portsmouth's High Street before leading his 22 ships of the line to face the combined French and Spanish fleets at Trafalgar.

The footpath leads you past Governor's Green and the Royal Garrison church. The church was bombed in the last war and the ruined nave has been left. Fortunately the 13th century chancel was saved and is still a consecrated church. Originally the church was part of the Domus Dei, a shelter for travellers and pilgrims, the sick and the elderly, founded by the Bishop of Winchester in 1212. At the Dissolution, in 1540, the hospice became the residence of the military Governor of Portsmouth. This was demolished in 1827, apart from the infirmary hall and the chapel which form the Royal

Garrison church.

Turn left to walk up to the top of the Long Curtain. The arrow-shaped platform on your left is King's Bastion. This was the flag base for the fortress and until 1931 it was the scene of the sunset ceremony of firing a gun and lowering the flag. Walk to the end of the Long Curtain enjoying an overall view of Spithead, and look for a concealed flight of steps just over a gravelled area on your right. These lead you down to Grand Parade and your car.

Before leaving, you might like to look at some of the interesting buildings that have survived the bombing in Old Portsmouth High Street. St Thomas's Cathedral dates from the 12th century and contains many treasures including a fragment of the white ensign flown by HMS *Victory* at Trafalgar and a plaque by Andrea della Robbia. John Pound's house was destroyed in the last war but a memorial chapel has been built on the site.

## Historical Notes

**Portsmouth (Solent Way):** Since earliest times Portsmouth Harbour had been valued as a convenient base for assembling a fleet for trade and military purposes. The Romans rowed their galleys to anchor under the protection of their fort at Portchester. The Normans constructed their castle at Portchester which remained a royal stronghold, well placed to supervise the increase in cross-channel trade. In the 12th century a small town developed around the Camber, a natural inlet at the mouth of the harbour, fortified by Edward III during the Hundred Years' War. For many centuries this remained the heart of Portsmouth's military garrison.

In 1495, Henry VII established the earliest known dry dock near the site of No 2 Dock, where HMS *Victory* now rests, to service his small fleet of warships. So began Portsmouth's long history as a naval base and dockyard.

**The Historic Ships:** HMS *Victory* is the longest-serving ship in the world, still commissioned as the flagship of the Commander-in-Chief, Naval Home Command. Recently she has been joined by HMS *Warrior*, the first iron-clad, iron-hulled warship, launched in 1860 and the pride of Queen Victoria's navy. The hull of Henry VIII's favourite warship, the *Mary Rose*, has been raised from the sea bed and is now on view, along with many everyday utensils found aboard her.

Portsmouth Naval Heritage, including the Historic Ships and the Royal Naval Museum, is open November to February 10.30 am to 5.30 pm, March to October 10 am to 6 pm.

**D-Day Museum:** The museum tells the story of D-Day with films, displays and tableaux and the remarkably accurate and detailed Overlord Embroidery. For up to date information on timings, admission charges and facilities ring 0705 296906.

**Southsea Castle:** Although the castle was never actually engaged in warfare, it has an eventful history. Its gunners were ready when in 1545 a fleet of 225 French ships was sighted off the Isle of Wight. The English fleet led by their pride, the *Mary Rose*, sailed out to meet them. Henry VIII stood watching from Southsea Castle. No battle took place but suddenly, under Henry's horrified gaze, the *Mary Rose* heeled over and sank, possibly because she was overloaded.

During the Civil War, Captain Chaloner held the castle for the King but was forced to surrender by a force of 400 Roundheads without a shot being fired. This was hardly surprising as his garrison consisted of 12 men and a dog!

The castle was manned during both world wars but was released by the Ministry of Defence in 1960. It is now a museum with an intriguing underground tunnel, much appreciated by children.

The castle is open daily March to October 10 am to 5.30 pm, November to February 10 am to 4.30 pm.

**Southsea Common:** The large area of Southsea Common was once a marsh popular with snipe shooters. Flattened and drained in the mid 19th century it was used by the military garrison for parades and exercises and as an assembly place for troops embarking for the Continent. Although belonging to the military, the local residents regarded it as common land and in 1874 this point was disputed at the 'Battle of Southsea Common' when the people faced the army and police and demanded rights of access. No one was seriously hurt and the people won!

In 1923 the City Council purchased the common from the War

Department but even then building was not allowed on the common as the field of fire from the batteries had to be kept clear. During the Second World War the common was the site for anti-aircraft guns and rocket batteries. Today it is Portsmouth's most extensive public open space, with gardens and sports facilities.

**HMS *Dolphin*: Royal Naval Submarine Museum (Solent Way):** This museum offers the unique opportunity to be guided by submariners around HMS *Alliance*, a patrol class vessel which stands on piles above the water. On exhibit also is the Navy's first submarine, *Holland I*. There is car parking and the museum is open daily 10 am to 4.30 pm including weekends. Refreshments are available.

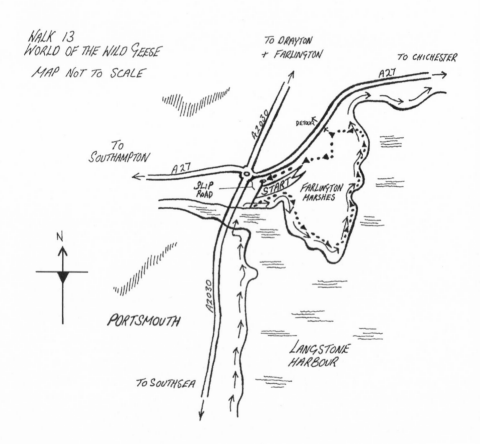

WALK 13
WORLD OF THE WILD GEESE

MAP NOT TO SCALE

TO DRAYTON
+ FARLINGTON

TO CHICHESTER

A27

A2030

TO SOUTHAMPTON

A27

DETOUR

SLIP
ROAD

START

FARLINGTON
MARSHES

N

A2030

PORTSMOUTH

LANGSTONE
HARBOUR

TO SOUTHSEA

# World of the wild geese – Farlington Marshes

## (Solent Way – Southsea Castle to Farlington Marshes <north-east>)

**Introduction:** The lonely expanse of Farlington Marshes stretching into the northern waters of Langstone Harbour is one of the finest nature reserves on the south coast. It is a magical place, especially during the winter months when great flocks of Brent geese arrive from the Arctic to feed on the saltings and rough pastures, filling the air with the beat of their heavy wings. But throughout the year the shallow mudflats washed by the tide attract vast numbers of birds including oyster-catchers, redshank, ringed plovers, dunlin and the striking black and white bar-tailed godwits.

And apart from the attraction of the tidal harbour, there is a wide variety of other habitats including a lagoon and freshwater streams, extensive reed beds, and lightly grazed pasture. The grassland is dotted with brambles and thorns and as it has seldom or never been ploughed it is rich in wild grasses and flowers.

The walk follows the coastal footpath round the marshes from which you can enjoy the wildlife of most of these differing areas and then returns by a shorter route which turns inland to explore the grasslands.

This is a short, easy walk, suitable for all the family. Don't forget your binoculars!

**Distance:** Southsea Castle to Farlington Marshes (north-east) on the Solent Way 8 miles. Circular walk 3 miles. OS Landranger series 1:50 000 maps 196 and 197. Using two maps can be awkward so I would recommend OS Pathfinder 1:25 000 map 1304.

**Refreshments:** There are no refreshment facilities at Farlington Marshes so it is a good idea to take a snack with you.

**How to get there:** Access is directly off the A27 (M27 westbound). Approaching from the west do not follow the M275 for Portsmouth but continue in the direction of Chichester and Havant. Turn left on the A2030 in the direction of Southsea. Look carefully as you go round the roundabout for a small slip road with a green board indicating Farlington Marshes, just before the A2030 turns left for Southsea – it is not easy to spot. You need to turn sharply left into the slip road as the entrance is very narrow. The parking area is immediately on your right, facing the harbour. If there is no room continue down the slip road where there are more parking areas.

Approaching from the east along the A27 turn at the roundabout for Southsea and turn sharp left down the slip road as directed above. Parking and access are free.

Portsmouth City Buses run services from the Hard near the Dockyard to Eastern Road close to Farlington Marshes.

**Solent Way – Southsea Castle to Farlington Marshes (north-east):** Southsea Castle is on your left as you follow the promenade along the sea front towards South Parade pier. Just beyond the pier and the canoe lake stand the remains of Lumps Fort beside the rose garden. Ahead, beyond Eastney Point, is the western shore of Hayling Island and the narrow entrance to Langstone Harbour. Continue past the entrance to the Royal Marines Museum with its impressive memorial to the marines who took part in the Falklands campaign in 1982 – a statue of a 'yomper'.

The Way follows the main road left, over a road to the ferry, and then continues to a T-junction. Turn left, keeping to the main road (Henderson Road) to pass Eastney Pumping Station. Two beam engines are housed in their original building, inscribed with the date, 1887. You can glimpse part of the machinery from the road, though the station is not open at the time of writing.

A few yards past the Pumping Station turn right to follow a footpath over a park. Keep on down the road ahead and bear right in front of St James' Hospital. When the road bends left, just past the Old Oyster House pub, keep straight on down a narrow footpath to the shore of Langstone Harbour. To the right of the path a small iron bridge crosses a remaining section of the canal that once connected Arundel with Portsmouth. The part of Milton sea lock which you see was constructed in 1822. The canal did not prosper and fell into disuse. From the bridge there is a fine view of a broken caisson, intended to form part of a Mulberry harbour, that has become stranded on Sinah Sands.

Turn left to follow a very pleasant coastal path beside the western shore of Langstone Harbour, past Great Salterns, once the site of a large area of saltworks, to the bridge over Ports Creek. Over the bridge turn right, then almost immediately right again following the sign for Farlington Marshes. Follow the route of Walk Thirteen as far as the north-east corner of the marshes, then turn to Walk Fourteen.

**The Walk:** Walk over the grass from the car park to the sea wall and turn left along the wall with the wide expanse of Langstone Harbour on your right. The view over the bird-haunted saltings and quiet water, only deep enough for small boats, forms a sharp contrast with Portsmouth Harbour. At high tide the water laps the wall and fronds of eelgrass – zostera – can be seen waving beneath it. As the water recedes it leaves behind a green algae. Both are the favourite food of the Brent geese, easily recognised by their sooty black heads and necks and small white nick behind each cheek. As the tide rises, many fly over the wall to roost on the short turf of the more heavily grazed grassland.

At the end of the parking area, bear left for a few yards before turning right past the reserve entrance to rejoin the sea wall. The low-lying pastures on your left are the oldest part of the reserve, probably enclosed 2,000 years ago. There is free access to this part of the reserve and we explore part of it on our return route. The path crosses the line of the Old Bank, the ancient sea wall, to continue along the sea wall built to encircle the marshes enclosed for rough grazing in the 18th century.

The path leads you by a small lagoon. This is fed by a freshwater creek so there is an interesting mix of birds, plants and animals. The salty areas that slope down to the lagoon are covered in mats of glasswort, vivid red in winter, sea asters, mud rushes and saltmarsh grass. Higher slopes have dense thickets of sedges where reed-warblers and reed-buntings breed, and in autumn and early winter you may see bearded tits, lovely little birds with tawny orange bodies and long tails flying over the reeds on rapidly whirring wings.

In the harbour, vast numbers of waders probe the mud of the saltings with their long beaks seeking food at different levels. Some of the islands you can see across the water are important breeding sites for ringed plovers and little terns and are protected by the RSPB.

If you walk these marshes in summer you may not see so many birds but you will be compensated by the wild flowers, some of them rare in other parts of the country. Golden samphire, with its bright daisy-like flowers, sea clover, and the crimson flowered grass vetchling grow beside the sea wall and along the edges of creeks and banks.

After the lagoon, the path leads over the most important part of the reserve. The grass is kept short by more intensive grazing to provide breeding sites for lapwings, redshanks and skylarks. You should see the dark shapes of short-eared owls which hunt by day outlined against the winter sky and perhaps rarer predators such as hobbies or merlins.

The path leads round the southernmost tip of the marshes, past the old oyster beds, and wide areas of saltmarsh, to a gate close to the reserve's north-east corner. Here the walk leaves the Solent Way. Do not go through the gate, but turn left down some steps and over a stile. Follow the path over the grass, close to a fence on the left. This leads to a gate. Past the gate, our route is left, but first I would suggest a short detour to discover a delightful area which should appeal especially to children.

Turn right and follow the track which tunnels under the A27. Go past the gate on the other side and turn immediately left to follow a narrow path for just a few yards. In front of you, fringed by rushes and flag irises, is Peter's Pond, one of several small lakes fed by freshwater streams and rich in wildlife.

Retrace your steps and continue down the track. When the track divides, bear right towards the warden's hut. Benches inside provide a sheltered place to rest. Opposite the hut is the ancient grassland with free access, so you might like to go past the gate ahead and ramble across this fascinating area in the direction of the reserve entrance. This is my favourite part of the reserve. The short turf is crossed by little winding creeks and dotted with ponds. Rabbits scurry for cover under thickets of brambles and hawthorns. Plants thrive in these natural conditions, especially grasses, and among the low growing shrubs you will find the pink flowers of restharrow, shaped like miniature sweet peas. All our familiar birds of field and hedgerow are here and in winter, flocks of fieldfares and redwings arrive from Scandinavia to enjoy the hawthorn berries.

Turn left from the reserve entrance to retrace your steps along the sea wall to your car.

## Historical Notes

**Langstone Harbour:** This is the quietest and most remote of the harbours of the Solent Way. It was once a coastal plain, flooded by rising sea levels as the ice melted over 12,000 years ago. Before the plain was flooded it was inhabited by farming and hunting communities whose flint tools are frequently found in the marshes and mudflats.

The harbour is shallow, almost drying out at low tide. In the past the few narrow creeks were the haunt of smugglers and pirates. Today they provide pleasant anchorages for small boats. This remoteness has led to Langstone Harbour, and especially Farlington Marshes, becoming one of the most important wintering areas for birds on the south coast. And, with over 15 miles of coastline, most of which is accessible for the walker, it is the perfect area from which to watch them.

Farlington Marshes are owned by Portsmouth City Council and looked after by the Hampshire and Isle of Wight Naturalists' Trust. For more information ring 0794 513786 or 830070.

**Royal Marines Museum (Solent Way):** Housed in the former officers' mess of the Eastney Barracks this museum tells the story of the Royal Marines from 1664 to the present day with dramatic displays and audio-visual effects. Among many exhibits are relics from the Falklands campaign, a chilling display of Arctic warfare, and a talking head of Hannah Snell, a female marine who remained undetected for five years. The museum is open daily 10 am to 5.30 pm Whitsun to August, 10 am to 4.30 pm September to May. There is a large car park.

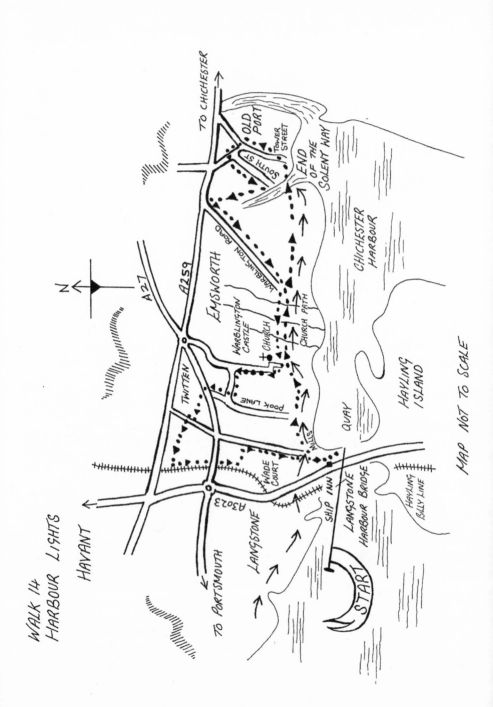

WALK 14
HARBOUR LIGHTS

MAP NOT TO SCALE

TO CHICHESTER

OLD PORT

TOWER STREET

SOUTH ST

END OF THE SOLENT WAY

CHICHESTER HARBOUR

WARBLINGTON ROAD

EMSWORTH

A259

A27

N

WARBLINGTON CASTLE

CHURCH

CHURCH PATH

POOK LANE

TWITTEN

HAYLING ISLAND

MILLS

QUAY

WADE COURT

A3023

LANGSTONE

HAVANT

TO PORTSMOUTH

SHIP INN

LANGSTONE HARBOUR BRIDGE

HAYLING BILLY LINE

START

# Harbour lights –
# Langstone and Emsworth

(Solent Way – Farlington Marshes <north-east>
to Emsworth)

**Introduction:** The final section of the Solent Way is included in this circular walk between two fascinating and very different shoreside villages. The walk starts from the quay at Langstone, the former port for Havant, a picturesque cluster of old cottages and inns, and continues to Emsworth, once famous for its oysters and tide mills and now a busy yachting centre, at the head of the western channel of Chichester Harbour. We take a closer look at both villages and explore Warblington which has a church dating back to Saxon times and a ruined castle once the home of Margaret Countess of Salisbury, the last of the Plantagenets.

The return route has a few surprises. These include an opportunity to walk down a 'twitten' and a nostalgic reminder of the days of steam as we take a short stroll down the track of the former 'Hayling Billy' line.

**Distance:** Farlington Marshes (north-east) to Emsworth on the Solent Way 6 miles. Circular walk 5 miles. OS Landranger Series 1:50 000 map 197 Chichester and the Downs.

**Refreshments:** Two inns, the Ship and the Royal Oak, on Langstone waterfront. All facilities beside the route in Emsworth, including several inns serving meals.

**How to get there:** From the A27, Portsmouth-Chichester road, take the A3023 signposted for Hayling Island. Langstone is ½ mile down this road and the parking area is just before the bridge, on the left in front of the Ship Inn. Parking is free. Buses from Portsmouth stop close by.

**Solent Way – Farlington Marshes (north-east) to Emsworth:** From the north-east corner of the marshes continue past the gate along the path fringed with gorse and broom. The path bears right to follow the coast. Cross a parking area and go over a public hard before bearing left beside a small creek. A bridge takes the Way over the A27 to a path which leads to a bridge over the railway, just south of Old Bedhampton. The Way turns left just before the bridge to bear right and run beneath it. Over the field on your right is Old Mill House. John Keats walked here along the coast road from Chichester in 1819 to stay with the miller. He was kept in with a sore throat and passed the time writing the final stanzas of *The Eve of St Agnes*. Continue beside the railway, turn right in front of a brick wall and after a few yards, bear left. The Hermitage stream is on your right and the Way crosses it over an iron bridge. Immediately, look for two stiles on your right, cross, and then walk diagonally across the field ahead. Go over the road and follow the path as it bears left then up steps to a bridge over the A27. Turn right and at the next road, bear right for just a few yards to cross to a footpath on the left running beside a stream. A bridge on the site of an old mill mentioned in the Domesday Book takes you to the side of the creek and past a large working wharf.

The path curves round the shore with wide views of Langstone Harbour and follows the sea wall skirting South Moor. Follow the wall left beside a creek, past a brick bridge, to turn right over the next bridge (site of a demolished mill) and continue along Mill Lane with the houses on your left. This takes you to the main road, the A3023. Cross and follow the road ahead, Langstone High Street, to join the route of Walk Fourteen at the house on its southern corner, known as the Winkle Market (see p. 121). Follow Walk Fourteen to the end of the Solent Way on the quay beside Emsworth Slipper Sailing Club.

**The Walk:** From the car park on the quayside by the Ship Inn there is a fine view to Hayling Island over the channel linking Langstone and Chichester harbours. To start the walk, turn left along the foreshore with the Ship Inn on your left. You pass a prominent watchtower and a row of coastguards' cottages, reminders of Langstone's smuggling days. If the tide is not high, just before you come to the foot of the High Street, you will be able to see the raised route of the old Wadeway across to Hayling Island, marked by posts. This ancient road, once passable at low tide, was the only way to the island on foot until 1817. Then a canal was cut across it with the intention of linking Portsmouth and Arundel.

On the southern corner of the High Street is a small house known as the Winkle Market. Here the walk follows the route of the Solent Way to continue along the shore past the Royal Oak, an 18th century inn, reputedly haunted by a woman in white. Offshore lies the wreck of the *Langstone*, a coaster which for many years brought gravel from the Winner shingle bank to be unloaded at Langstone Quay.

The footpath curves right between a former tide mill and the mill pond. Close by stands the black tower of a windmill, which could be worked while the tide refilled the mill pond. This was converted into a dwelling house by the artist, Flora Twort, in 1932.

The path continues along the foreshore past the remains of a quay where coal barges once unloaded at the foot of Pook Lane, to a stile. Cross, and walk diagonally over the field ahead towards the corner of Warblington churchyard. Enter, and at the first cross path turn left. Take the third path on the right to make your way towards a brick building (a toilet block) in the north-east corner. Leave the churchyard by a gate, cross the lane and take the footpath ahead which runs to the right of Warblington church.

There are traces of Saxon work in the small central tower rising above the deep eaves of this attractive church. The rest of the building dates from the 12th and 13th centuries, apart from the north porch constructed of beautifully carved ships' timbers which was possibly built 100 years later. Now the church stands almost alone, half-hidden among trees, but once it was the centre of a village deserted after the Black Death. On the corner of the old graveyard you pass a curious brick and flint hut. This is one of two shelters for gravewatchers in the churchyard, built in the early 19th century to prevent body snatching. Evidently the watchers met with some success as one hut contains a lock-up. Beside the hut is an enormous yew tree, 1,500 years old. Inside the church is a certificate to prove it.

The path leads over fields and across a tiny, crystal clear stream full of watercress and the white flowers of brookweed. A little further on you cross another stream to enter an oak and hawthorn wood. A wide view of Chichester Harbour and Thorney Island opens before you as you leave the wood and approach Emsworth waterfront.

The old village, with its charming narrow streets, is built between two natural inlets which have been dammed to power tide mills, two on each inlet. Today, the mills have a variety of uses and the paths beside the mill ponds provide delightful walks and ample opportunities to feed the ducks and swans. The walk follows the Solent Way along Emsworth foreshore, to continue to the left of the most westerly mill (home of the Emsworth Sailing Club) and over a lane to follow a footpath sign leading to the sea wall built in 1760 to contain the western mill pond. The path follows the wall for over 200 yards as it curves round to meet the Town Mill (home of the Emsworth Slipper Sailing Club) on the other side of the inlet. Here, on the quay beside the mill, we come to the end of the Solent Way. Emsworth's 14 inns await the thirsty traveller.

The old port of Emsworth is captivating and the next part of the walk reveals a little of its special character. From the quay, turn right along the foreshore following the footpath sign. After about 100 yards look carefully for a flight of concrete steps leading between the harbour walls on your left. Climb these and follow the twisting lane into Tower Street, described by Pevsner as 'the most delicious inland backwater in Emsworth'. Regal Georgian houses with fanlit doorways and elegant iron balconies face each other across the narrow street. Only seconds away you emerge on the busy High Street – still old-fashioned enough to keep its small specialist shops. Turn left, then first left again to follow South Street as it slopes down to Town Mill. Rows of solid, colour-washed cottages, their deeply recessed doorways fitted with tide boards as they approach the waterfront, reveal other aspects of Emsworth as a fishing and shipbuilding village and, in common with most south coast villages in the past, a favourite haunt for smugglers.

With the Town Mill on your left, follow the road that bears right beside the westerly inlet (Bridgefoot Path). Follow this to the main road and turn left. After about 50 yards, turn left down Warblington

Road which quickly brings you back to the foreshore. Bear right to retrace your steps to Warblington church. Do not go through the new churchyard but turn right up the lane (church on your right). The lane bears left past a black barn, then right, with the ruins of Warblington Castle over the field on your right. Only the tower forming part of the gatehouse and an adjoining archway is left of the moated house built by the Countess of Salisbury between 1514 and 1526. Held for the King, the house fell into ruin after being slighted by Commonwealth troops during the Civil War.

Take the first turning on the left, Pook Lane, and when you come to a T-junction turn right towards the main road, A27. Cross by the bridge, and at the other side turn immediately left down a narrow path with a 'no cycling' sign. You are now walking down a twitten! This very straight route is one of several ancient rights of way that once crossed open countryside linking the Saxon settlements of Warblington, Langstone and Bedhampton with each other and with Havant. The twitten leads to a road. Look across, a few yards to your right, and you will see the twitten continuing by a telegraph pole. Keep on (past a path leading left) till you emerge on the track of the former branch line that ran from Havant to Hayling. The train that carried so many holiday-makers to the first holiday camps on the island became known as 'Hayling Billy'.

Bear left along the track, with the Lymbourne stream running through a deep cleft beside you. The track tunnels under the main road and shortly after look carefully for a small bridge over the stream on your left, leading towards Wade Court. Cross the bridge and walk over the field ahead to turn right down the lane past Wade Court with its conspicuous tower modelled on that of St Faith's church in Havant. The pretty lane sunk between knotted tree roots leads you back to the foreshore. Turn right to walk back to your car.

## Historical Notes

**Langstone:** The quays along the waterfront were once busy with local barges unloading their cargoes, principally of Hampshire grain. Langstone had three mills which were kept at full stretch supplying the dockyard at Portsmouth, with demand increasing dramatically during the Napoleonic wars. Another source of income, perhaps less praiseworthy, was smuggling. The meeting place was the Royal Oak Inn. So suspicious were the excise men that an old brig, the *Griper*, was permanently moored offshore with the coastguard aboard. No smuggler was ever caught.

**Warblington:** There is a real feeling of antiquity about the church and castle. The church is locked, but if you would like to see inside the key can be obtained from a cottage 100 yards up the road (see the church noticeboard).

Margaret Pole, Countess of Salisbury, could not, as a Catholic, approve of Henry VIII's divorce. By retiring to Warblington she hoped to escape the King's anger but at the age of 70 she was accused of treason and beheaded – standing, she refused to kneel as she said she was no traitor – on Tower Hill. The beautiful chantry built for her in Christchurch Priory remains empty.

**Emsworth:** Plenty of time is needed to appreciate this village. Apart from milling, Emsworth prospered on the oyster trade. They were brought from the east coast to be fattened in the many oyster beds in the harbour, the remains of which can still be seen today. Late in the 19th century J.D. Foster built a fleet of the famous Emsworth fishing smacks to dredge for them. Unfortunately, after a banquet at Winchester which included oysters from Emsworth, the Bishop of Winchester and some other guests died from typhus. So the oyster trade came to an end.

Another well known Emsworth shipbuilder was John King, and his fine weather-boarded house can be seen in King Street. Today the busy harbour is colourful with yachts and small boats and the beauty of Emsworth's surroundings is enjoyed by the village's many tourists including artists, naturalists and walkers.

## Further Reading

*Exploring Hampshire's Coast*, Hampshire County Recreation Department, 1991

*Hampshire's Countryside Heritage* No 7 The Coast, Hampshire County Council, 1984

*The Solent Way: a guide to Hampshire's Coast*, Barry Shurlock, Hampshire County Recreation Department, 1984

*The New Hampshire Village Book*, Countryside Books and the Hampshire Federation of Women's Institutes, Winchester, 1990

*It Happened in Hampshire* published by the Hampshire Federation of Women's Institutes

*The Bournemouth Coast Path*, Leigh Hatts, Countryside Books, 1985

*Hampshire Coast Ways*, S.L. Ritchie, Adlard Coles, 1958

*The New Forest*, J.R. Wise, S.R. Publishers, Reprint, 1971

*Explore Hampshire*, John H. Holder and Barry Shurlock, Hampshire County Recreation Department, 1986

*A Hampshire Treasury*, Margaret Green, Winton Publications, 1972

*Guide to Prehistoric England*, Nicholas Thomas

*The Solent*, R.L.P. and Dorothy M. Jowitt, Terence Dalton Ltd, 1978

*Hampshire Days*, W.H. Hudson, Barry Shurlock, 1973

*Hampshire and the Isle of Wight*, Pevsner and Lloyd, 1967

*Lymington*, Brian J. Down, Paul Cave Publications Ltd, 1989